Schülerhilfe®
Das Original. Seit 1974.

W0395794

# GUTE NOTEN IN ENGLISCH

## KLASSE 8

SABINE MEISINGER-BOTZ

tandem.VERLAG
print line

Zeichnungen: Sabine Völkers, Berlin
Layout: Cordula Schaaf, München
Texte S. 82 und 84f./122f.: Simon Tribe, Stralsund
Umschlagabbildung: michaeljung/fotolia
Umschlaggestaltung: [rincón]2 medien gmbh, Köln

www.tandem-verlag.de


Gesamtherstellung: Tandem Verlag GmbH, Potsdam

ISBN 978-3-8427-1204-1

# Contents

★ Dieses Sternchen markiert Übungen und Regeln, die etwas anspruchsvoller sind oder nicht überall verlangt werden. Wenn du ganz sicher bist, dass du sie nicht brauchst, kannst du sie überspringen. Ansonsten gilt: Stell dich der Herausforderung!

# 1 Revision of Tenses

Jenny and Peter Wilson are 16-year-old twins who live in London with their parents and their older brother Thomas. Peter is a gifted football player and Jenny loves singing and dancing, whereas Thomas can play the guitar really well. He attends the sixth form at his school and is planning a year abroad after his A-levels this summer. Last but not least, there is also Rex, the Wilsons' two-year-old German shepherd dog.

## 1.1 Revision of Present and Past Tenses

**Alles klar?!** ***Active** and **Passive** Forms and their Functions*

| ***Aspect* / *Tense*** | ***Simple*** | |
|---|---|---|
| ***Present*** | ***„he, she, it – das -s muss mit!"***<br>***am/is/are + past participle***<br><br><br>**Verwendung:**<br>• Gesetzmäßigkeiten und allgemeine Wahrheiten<br>• regelmäßig wiederholte Tätigkeiten<br>• Zustandsbeschreibungen<br>• Reihe aufeinanderfolgender Tätigkeiten | *The sun **rises** in the east.*<br>*Jenny **doesn't like** olives.*<br>*The thief **is caught, arrested** and **taken** to prison.*<br><br>**Signalwörter:**<br>*usually, often, sometimes, every day/week/…, always, occasionally, on Mondays* |
| ***Present Perfect*** | ***have/has + past participle***<br>***have/has + been + past participle***<br>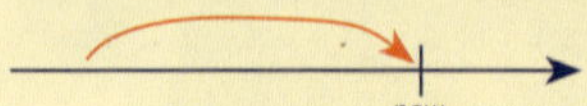<br><br>**Verwendung:**<br>• Handlung in der Vergangenheit, deren genauer Zeitpunkt unwichtig ist, deren Auswirkung auf die Gegenwart jedoch bedeutend ist oder betont wird<br>• Zustand, der in der Vergangenheit begonnen hat und bis zur Gegenwart andauert | *I **have lost** my keys.*<br>*It **has been** cold for two months now.*<br>***Has** the dog **been fed**?*<br><br>**Signalwörter:**<br>*for …, since …, before, all my life, already, ever, never, so far, up to now, (not) yet* |
| ***Past*** | ***-ed (or irregular form)***<br>***was/were + past participle***<br><br><br>**Verwendung:**<br>• in der Vergangenheit abgeschlossene Handlung<br>• Zeitpunkt des Geschehens wichtig | *We **watched** that film yesterday.*<br>*The car **was repaired** last week.*<br><br>**Signalwörter:**<br>*yesterday, in 1900, last week/month/ …, two years ago* |
| ***Past Perfect*** | ***had + past participle***<br>***had + been + past participle***<br>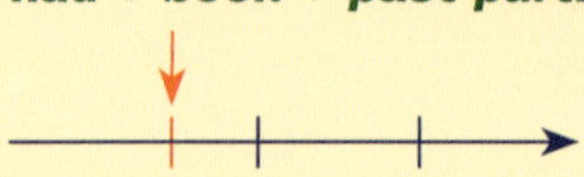<br><br>**Verwendung:**<br>• Handlung, die vor einem Zeitpunkt in der Vergangenheit stattgefunden hatte | *After Peter **had closed** the door, he realized that he **had left** the key inside.*<br>*The house **had been sold** before they arrived.*<br><br>**Signalwörter:**<br>*after, before* |

**Aufgepasst!**
**Zustandsverben** *(state verbs)* können nicht in der *progressive form*, sondern nur in der ***simple form*** einer Zeit stehen.
Beispiel: *Peter **knows** the rules.*

***Progressive***

---

***am/is/are + -ing***
***am/is/are + being + past participle***

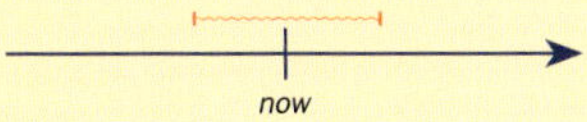


*Jenny is **doing** her homework (now).*
*The thief **is being questioned** at the moment.*

**Verwendung:**
- augenblicklich im Verlauf befindliche Handlung

**Signalwörter:**
*now, at the moment, still, Look! ..., Listen! ...*

---

***have/has + been + -ing***

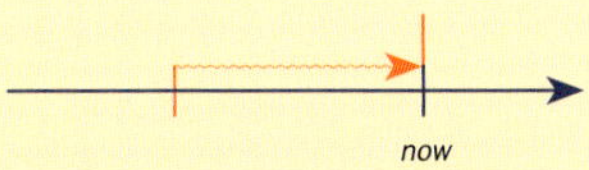


*I **have been waiting** for you since 8 o'clock.*

(**Anm.:** Das Passiv wird nicht verwendet.)

**Verwendung:**
- Handlung, die in der Vergangenheit begonnen hat und bis zur Gegenwart andauert
- Betonung der Dauer

**Signalwörter:**
*for ..., since ..., all day/night ..., the whole afternoon/day ..., how long?*

---

***was/were + -ing***
***was/were + being + past participle***

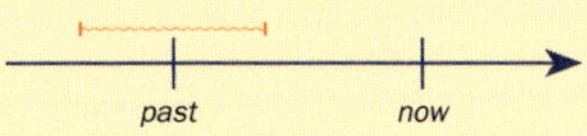


*We **were watching** TV when Jenny arrived.*
*While Mrs Wilson **was writing** an e-mail, the house **was being painted**.*

**Verwendung:**
- zu einem bestimmten Zeitpunkt in der Vergangenheit im Verlauf befindliche Handlung

**Signalwörter:**
*while*

---

***had + been + -ing***

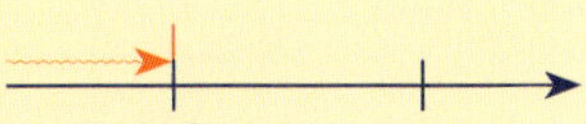


*She **had been living** in Berlin before she moved to Munich.*

(**Anm.:** Das Passiv wird nicht verwendet.)

**Verwendung:**
- Handlung, die vor einem Zeitpunkt in der Vergangenheit begonnen hatte und bis zu diesem andauerte

**Signalwörter:**
*when, before ..., by ...*

**Zur Erinnerung:**
Das *past participle* wird bei **regelmäßigen** Verben auf *-ed* gebildet. Bei **unregelmäßigen** Verben findest du es in der dritten Spalte der Verbtabellen und musst es auswendig lernen.

**Exercise 1** **Form sentences using the simple past and past progressive.**

1. When – Mrs Wilson – come home – from job interview – Mr Wilson – prepare – dinner

   ..........................................................................................................

2. Mr Wilson – peel – potatoes – when – his mobile phone – ring

   ..........................................................................................................

3. At 2 o'clock – Jenny – write – text message – to Anne – on her new mobile phone

   ..........................................................................................................

4. Thomas – must – lie down – because – have – a bad headache

   ..........................................................................................................

5. Rex – be – nervous – when – ambulance – drive – past

   ..........................................................................................................

**Exercise 2** **Put the verb into the correct tense.**

1. Jenny and Peter ............................................ (be) both in year 8 now.
   They ............................................ (choose) German as a foreign language.
2. Jenny's best friend Anne ............................................ (be) also in their class.
3. Thomas is in the sixth form; he ............................................ (study) for his A-levels.
4. Thomas ............................................ (never – be) to Canada, but
   he ............................................ (want) to go there after finishing school.
5. What ............................................ (he – do) last night at ten o'clock? –
   He ............................................ (play) the guitar.
6. Mrs Wilson ............................................ (look) for an interesting job since
   she ............................................ (lose) her job as a translator last year.
7. Apart from being a housewife at the moment, she ............................................ (start)
   a course for web page design six months ago.
8. Mr Wilson ............................................ (like) cooking and ............................................
   (promise) to prepare a roast turkey for tonight.



*Lösungen Seite 100*

## 1.2 Revision of Future Tenses

**Alles klar?!** ***Revision of Future Tenses – Active and Passive Forms***

***going-to-Future***

***am/is/are + going to + infinitive***
***am/is/are + going to + be + past participle***

*Thomas **is going to spend** a year abroad.*
*She **is going to have** a baby.*
*The meeting **is going to be held** on Friday.*

**Verwendung:**
- Pläne und Absichten
- mit hoher Wahrscheinlichkeit eintretendes Ereignis mit deutlichen Anzeichen

***will-Future***

***will + infinitive***
***will + be + past participle***

*There **will be** sunshine tomorrow.*
*It's raining; I **will take** you home in my car.*
*I think Peter **will be chosen** for the team.*

**Verwendung:**
- Vorhersagen und Annahmen (oft ohne Einflussmöglichkeit des Sprechers)
- spontane Entscheidungen, Angebote und Versprechen

**Zur Erinnerung:** *will + not = won't*

**Signalwörter:**
*I think/believe/expect/hope, I'm sure, perhaps, probably, maybe*

***Future Progressive***

***will + be + -ing***

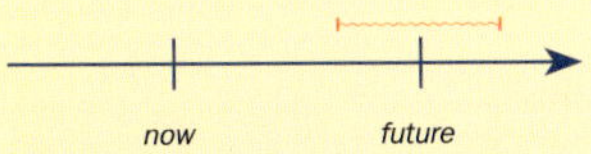


*This time tomorrow Thomas **will be taking** his English test.*
*On Friday Peter **will be playing** football as usual.*

**Verwendung:**
- zu einem bestimmten Zeitpunkt in der Zukunft im Verlauf befindliche Handlung
- wie gewohnt stattfindendes oder bereits feststehendes Ereignis

(**Anm.:** Das Passiv wird nicht verwendet.)

***Future Perfect***

***will + have + past participle***
***will + have + been + past participle***

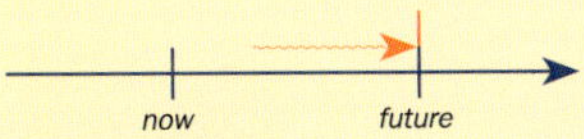


***Will** you **have finished** your homework by 5 o'clock?*
*This firm **will have been ruined** by this time next year.*

**Verwendung:**
- Handlung, die zu einem bestimmten Zeitpunkt in der Zukunft abgeschlossen sein wird

**Signalwörter:**
*by ..., this time next week/year/...*

**Alles klar?!** ***Present Tense with Future Meaning – Active and Passive Forms***

*Simple present* und *present progressive* können nicht nur Handlungen und Ereignisse in der Gegenwart (vgl. Kapitel 1.1), sondern auch zukünftige Geschehnisse ausdrücken:

***Simple Present***

***„he, she, it – das -s muss mit!"***
***am/is/are + past participle***

*The train **leaves** at 8.30.*
*The film **starts** at 8 pm.*

**Verwendung:**
- durch Fahrplan, Stundenplan, Programm, Terminplan festgelegtes Geschehen – daher auch ***timetable future*** genannt!

**Signalwörter:**
*arrive, leave, start, stop, begin*

***Present Progressive***

***am/is/are + -ing***
***am/is/are + being + past participle***

*Sorry, I can't join you because I **am playing** football with Peter tomorrow.*

**Verwendung:**
- fest geplantes Vorhaben, Verabredung

**Exercise** ★ **Put the verbs into the correct future tense.**

Jenny, Peter and their friends are talking about their holiday plans.

*Jenny:* I think I ................................ (get) a holiday job at a café. I ................................ (ask) at several cafés in the neighbourhood. I ................................ (take) part in a dancing workshop in summer; my parents have lent me the money for it. It ................................ (start) in June, and perhaps I ................................ (win) the competition in August.

*Peter:* I ................................ (probably – do) an extra maths course. I know that ................................ (not be) much fun, but it's necessary. Apart from that I ................................ (play) football whenever possible. On Friday 5th, Chelsea ................................ (play), and I've got tickets! So from about 8 pm I ................................ (sit) in the stadium.

*Anne:* I ................................ (join) my cousin Jill on her trip to Spain; my parents have allowed it! My mother ................................ (have) a baby, so she ................................ (not travel) a lot this year. But by next year, we ................................ (all – get used) to the baby, so maybe we ................................ (fly) to Greece then.

*Tim:* I ................................ (take) part in a circus project. It ................................ (take) place in the first holiday week, from 9 am to 4 pm every day. We ................................ (train) all week long, and the performance ................................ (start) at 3 pm on Saturday. My parents and friends ................................ (come) to watch it. Do you also want to see it?



*Lösungen Seite 100*

## Test your Progress (30 minutes)

**Exercise 1** **Fill in the right tenses of the verbs.**

1. Uncle Harry ................................... (live – always) in Liverpool.
2. Mrs Wilson ................................... (buy) a new hat. Isn't it beautiful?
3. On June 5th in the morning, Thomas ................................... (take) his A-levels in maths.
4. ................................... (you – play) football when you were a boy?
5. Peter ................................... (lie) in hospital when his father ................................... (buy) the new car last Saturday.
6. The plane ................................... (take off – just); it ................................... (be) in New York in 7 hours.
7. While Mrs Wilson ................................... (make) the cake yesterday, Jenny ................................... (do) her homework.
8. I ................................... (read) this book soon.

Points: ☐ out of 11

**Exercise 2** **Choose the correct verb and fill it in using the right tense.**

*hear – not come – be – visit – practise – climb – tell (2x) – wait – walk – go (2x)*

Last weekend Peter ............................ his Uncle Harry in Liverpool. Now he ............................ Jenny about it. "I ............................ Uncle Harry that I would arrive at 11 am, but then my train was late. Fortunately, he ............................ at the station when I finally arrived. We ............................ to the Cathedral, where I ............................ to the top. Uncle Harry ............................ there so many times that he ............................ with me; he had a coffee at the Cathedral coffee shop instead. I ............................ a lot about the Beatles' first concerts, so we also ............................ to see the famous Cavern Club, where a band ............................ for a concert. I hope we ............................ there again on my next visit."

Points: ☐ out of 12

*Lösungen Seite 100/101*

**Exercise 3** **Put the verbs into the correct tense.**

Jenny, Peter and Thomas are planning their weekend.

*Thomas:* .................................... (you – decide – yet) what you want to do on Saturday, Peter?

*Peter:* Well, I .................................... (talk) to Aunt Helen on the phone yesterday, and she .................................... (say) she would like to come over.

*Jenny:* Probably the weather .................................... (be) nice. So we could take her on a walk to the National Gallery and show her the painting exhibition.

*Peter:* I think there ............................ (not be) enough time, as her train .................................... (arrive) at half past four and the exhibition .................................... (end) at five o'clock.

*Jenny:* That's a pity. How about a party for Aunt Helen? We .................................... (not see) her for months, and it .................................... (be) her birthday anyway.

*Peter:* How old .................................... (she – be)?

*Jenny:* 45, I think.

*Thomas:* Well, perhaps I .................................... (paint) a picture of her as a surprise present.

*Peter:* But be careful, she .................................... (be) rather angry if the picture isn't good.

*Jenny:* How about visiting Greenwich and the Royal Observatory on Sunday? I .................................... (read) a book about its history at the moment, and it .................................... (sound) really interesting.

*Peter:* .................................... (you – be – ever) there, Thomas?

*Thomas:* Oh, yes, I .................................... (be) there when I was little, but I can hardly remember. So why not go there?

*Jenny:* That sounds good. I think it .................................... (be) an interesting weekend!

Points: ☐ out of 17

Total points: ☐ out of 40

36–40: Super! Du beherrschst die Zeiten schon sehr gut!
20–35: Teilweise kannst du die Aufgaben schon recht gut lösen, aber oft machst du noch Fehler. Schau dir die Regeln noch einmal an und wiederhole die Übungen, bei denen du Probleme hattest.
0–19: Die richtige Verwendung der Zeiten bereitet dir noch große Probleme. Wiederhole die Regeln gründlich und mache die Übungen konzentriert noch einmal.


*Lösungen Seite 101*

# 2 Conditional Sentences

Jenny and her friend Anne are members of the local youth club. They used to go there once a week to meet friends, play games or dance in the club's disco room. However, recently Jenny has tried to get there more often in order to meet Richard, a boy she fancies. She wonders what would happen if she asked him to go to the cinema with her.

## 2.1 Conditional Sentences – Types I, II and III

**Alles klar?!** ***Conditional Sentences – Type I***

Die Bedingung, die im if-Satz genannt wird, ist realistisch und erfüllbar.

| ***if-Clause*** | ***Main Clause*** |
|---|---|
| *simple present* | *will-future/modal auxiliary/imperative* |
| *If I **go** to the club,* | *I **will see** him.* |
| *If you **do** your homework properly,* | *you **may go out** in the evening.* |
| *If you **go** shopping,* | ***bring** me some sugar, please.* |

**Merke!**
Situationsabhängig kann im **if-Satz** auch das *present perfect* stehen:
*If Jenny **has missed** the bus,*
*she **will be** late for the first lesson.*

Bei allgemeingültigen Aussagen steht im **Hauptsatz** anstatt des *will-future* das *simple present*:
*If the temperatures **are** cold enough,*
*rain **turns** into snow.*

**Exercise 1** **Put in the correct verb forms. Some of the sentences will make more sense if you use an auxiliary!**

1. If you .............................. (come) to the club, we .............................. (meet).
2. If Anne .............................. (go) there, too, Jenny .............................. (show) Richard to her.
3. It .............................. (rain) if they .............................. (leave) very late.
4. If it .............................. (rain) too much, Richard .............................. (not come).
5. .............................. I .............................. (recognize) him if I .............................. (not wear) my glasses?
6. If you .............................. (finish) your homework soon, .............................. (help) me in the kitchen, please.
7. Anne .............................. (help) Jenny with German if she .............................. (need) her.
8. If Thomas .............................. (pass) his maths test, he .............................. (go) on a weekend trip with his friends.

 *Lösungen Seite 101*

**Alles klar?!** ***Conditional Sentences – Type II***

Die Bedingung ist nur theoretisch erfüllbar bzw. die Erfüllung ist eher unwahrscheinlich.

| ***if-Clause*** | ***Main Clause*** |
|---|---|
| *simple past* | *would/could/might + infinitive* |
| *If I **went** to the club,* | *I **would see** him.* |
| *If you **did** your exercises properly,* | *you **could pass** the text.* |
| *If Peter **was** working hard,* | *he **might** even **get** a good mark.* |

**Exercise 2** **Choose the correct verb form.**

1. If you know/knew Richard, you would agree/agreed that he is really handsome.
2. You would catch/caught the bus if you leave/left in time.
3. If Thomas took/take driving lessons, he would drive/could drive a car.
4. If Jenny thought/thinks reasonably, she ate/would eat something.
5. It would be/will be better if you waited/would wait for me.
6. Jenny comes/would come if Richard would invite/invited her.
7. If the youth club will be closed/was closed, what did/would we do?
8. If Mr Wilson would play/played the lottery, he might win/won a million.

**Merke!**
Situationsabhängig kann im if-Satz auch das *past progressive* stehen.

*If Jenny **was telling** a lie, her mother **would notice** immediately.*

**Übrigens!**
Im Bedingungssatz Typ II kann im formellen Englisch anstatt *was* auch *were* stehen. Häufig findet man diese Form in Sätzen wie „*If I **were** you, …*“, z. B.:
*If I **were** a bird, I **would** fly in the sky.*

*Lösungen Seite 102*

**Alles klar?!** ***Conditional Sentences – Type III***

Die Bedingung bezieht sich auf die Vergangenheit und ist daher nicht mehr erfüllbar.

| ***if-Clause*** | ***Main Clause*** |
|---|---|
| *past perfect* | *would/could/might + have + past participle* |
| *If I **had gone** to the club,*<br>*If we **had known** about your problem,*<br>*If Mr Wilson **had won** the lottery,* | *I **would have seen** him.*<br>*we **could have helped** you.*<br>*he **might have bought** a diamond for his wife.* |

**Aufgepasst!**
Das ***conditional*** steht **nie** im if-Satz!
- *conditional simple =* ***would*** *+ infinitive*
- *conditional perfect =* ***would*** *+ have + past participle*

**Merke!**
Die Kurzform ***'d*** kann für verschiedene Wörter stehen:
*If I'**d gone** to the club, ...* → *'d = had*
*... we'**d have met**.* → *'d = would*

**Exercise 3** **Join the sentences using a conditional sentence type III.**

*Example: Anne didn't find the birthday card. She didn't look into her bag.*
***Anne would have found the birthday card if she had looked into her bag.***

1. Richard forgot Jenny's birthday. He didn't invite her to the cinema.

   ...........................................................................................................................

2. Peter didn't learn enough English. He failed the test.

   ...........................................................................................................................

3. Thomas was not at home before midnight. His parents were angry.

   ...........................................................................................................................

4. Anne broke into the frozen river. She wasn't careful.

   ...........................................................................................................................

5. You didn't ask me. I couldn't help you.

   ...........................................................................................................................

6. Thomas didn't see the bus. He was injured in an accident.

   ...........................................................................................................................



*Lösungen Seite 102*

**Exercise 4** **Join the sentences.**

*Example:*

*1.–2. If Anne had caught the bus to the youth club, Jenny would have met her there.*

1. Anne didn't catch the bus to the youth club.
2. Jenny didn't meet her there.
3. They didn't go to the cinema together.
4. Thomas was not waiting for them there.
5. He didn't ask Anne to go out with him.
6. They didn't spend a wonderful evening together.
7. She didn't come home after midnight.
8. She didn't oversleep the next day.

2.–3. If Jenny had met ......................................................

3.–4. ......................................................

4.–5. ......................................................

5.–6. ......................................................

6.–7. ......................................................

7.–8. ......................................................

**Exercise 5** ★ **Put in the correct verb form. Keep all three types of conditional sentences in mind!**

1. If Peter's friend Daniel from Munich .......................... (come) for a visit next summer, the Wilsons .......................... (show) him all the famous sights in London.
2. If Daniel's parents came, too, Mr and Mrs Wilson .......................... (take) them to one of the many theatres in the West End to see a musical.
3. "We .......................... (walk) through Hyde Park if the weather .......................... (be) fine; if you ever .......................... (get) lost, just .......................... (look) at this map."
4. If Daniel .......................... (be) interested in arts, they .......................... (can – visit) the Tate Modern, a great gallery of modern art.
5. They .......................... (make – can) a trip to Brighton on the south coast if Daniel stayed for more than a week.
6. "If I .......................... (be) you, I .......................... (stay) here for at least one month."
7. If Daniel .......................... (know) that staying with the Wilsons was so much fun, he .......................... (visit) them earlier.

*Lösungen Seite 102*

## 2.2 Conditional Sentences – Mixed Types

**Alles klar?!** ***Conditional Sentences – Mixed Types***

Situationsabhängig gibt es auch Mischformen, d. h. Konditionalsätze, die aus den drei Grundtypen kombiniert sind.

| ***if-Clause*** | ***Main Clause*** |
| --- | --- |
| *past tense*<br>*If Thomas **wasn't** so clever,* | *conditional perfect*<br>*he **wouldn't have passed** that difficult test.* |
| *past perfect*<br>*If Peter **had not waited** for Tom in the rain,* | *conditional simple*<br>*he **would not have** a cold now.* |
| *past tense*<br>*If you **made** no mistake in your maths test,* | *will-future*<br>*you **will get** a very good mark.* |

**Exercise** ★ **Complete the sentences translating the missing parts.**

1. Peter wouldn't be such a good football player ..........................................
   .......................... *(wenn er nicht mit vier Jahren zu spielen angefangen hätte).*
2. If Jenny wasn't a talented dancer, ..........................................
   .......................... *(hätte sie nicht am Workshop teilnehmen können).*
3. If Anne left home only three minutes ago, ..........................................
   .......................... *(wird sie zu spät zur Schule kommen).*
4. *(Wenn Mr Wilson keinen Unfall gehabt hätte)* ..........................................
   .........................., he wouldn't have a broken leg now.
5. *(Ich bin sicher, Richard hätte Jenny eingeladen)* ..........................................
   .......................... if he knew her better.
6. If Peter was more reliable, ..........................................
   .......................... *(hätte er sich das Rad seines Bruders ausleihen können).*
7. *(Wenn Mr Wilson den Ring gekauft hätte)* ..........................................
   .........................., he would have a birthday present for his wife now.
8. *(Wenn das Geschäft um 6 Uhr geschlossen hat)* ..........................................
   .........................., we won't get any salt-and-vinegar crisps for the party tonight.



*Lösungen Seite 103*

## Test your Progress (25 minutes)

**Exercise 1** **Mark the correct constructions. There may be more than one correct solution.**

| | | |
|---|---|---|
| If I lend you the money, | you will spend it on clothes. | ❏ |
| | you spent it on clothes. | ❏ |
| | you would have spent it on clothes. | ❏ |
| You would not be at the party | if I did not invite you. | ❏ |
| | if I had not invited you. | ❏ |
| | if I would not have invited you. | ❏ |
| If you want to be successful, | you might work hard. | ❏ |
| | you will have to work hard. | ❏ |
| | you would have to work hard. | ❏ |
| If Peter wanted to go to the football match, | his father would take him there. | ❏ |
| | his father took him there. | ❏ |
| | his father will take him there. | ❏ |
| Jenny only asks her mother for advice | if she was not sure herself. | ❏ |
| | if she is not sure herself. | ❏ |
| | if she had not been sure herself. | ❏ |
| Would Jenny and Anne have become friends | if they lived in the same house? | ❏ |
| | if they live in the same house? | ❏ |
| | if they had lived in the same house? | ❏ |
| If you try hard, | you may become a famous dancer. | ❏ |
| | you will become a famous dancer. | ❏ |
| | you would become a famous dancer. | ❏ |

Points: ☐ out of 9

**Exercise 2** **Cross out the wrong verb forms.**

1. Jenny and Anne, if you walk/walked/will walk all the way home in the middle of the night, something terrible happened/happens/might happen.
2. Peter, if you stay/will stay/would stay at the disco after midnight, the police are taking/take/will take you home.
3. What did/will/would you do if a stranger asked/will ask/would ask you where you were going?
4. If my mother asked/asks/would ask me to do all the housework, I am moving/moved/would move out!
5. If a stranger might offer/had offered/would offer me some chocolate when I was a child, I certainly didn't take/wouldn't take/wouldn't have taken it.
6. I ran/will run/would run away if my parents told/will tell/would tell me to marry a rich man.

*Lösungen Seite 103/104*

7. If Mr and Mrs Wilson didn't meet/hadn't met/wouldn't meet at a party 20 years ago, Thomas, Jenny and Peter weren't/won't be/wouldn't have been born.
8. If you joined/join/will join the youth club, you can come/will come/have been able to come to the disco every week."

Points: ☐ out of 16

**Exercise 3** **Put in the correct verb form.**

1. Anne .................................... (buy) those jeans if they were not so expensive.
2. If the weather .................................... (be) fine, I will play tennis.
3. If you .................................... (read) the instructions before, you would know how to use the camera.
4. If the pupils .................................... (be) attentive, there won't be any homework.
5. If he doesn't shut the window, we .................................... (die) of cold.
6. Peter .................................... (be killed) if the bus hadn't stopped.
7. If Mrs Wilson .................................... (know) how to work with the computer, she wouldn't have had so many job interviews yet.
8. If you .................................... (want) to have dinner soon, lay the table, please.
9. Mum would be very angry with us if we .................................... (take) her mobile phone without asking.
10. Call before ten o'clock if you .................................... (want) me to drive you home.
11. If the telephone .................................... (ring), the cake wouldn't have been burnt.
12. If I succeed in the exam, I .................................... (be) very proud!

Points: ☐ out of 12

Total points: ☐ out of 37

34–37: Super! Du beherrschst die Bedingungssätze schon sehr gut!
19–33: Teilweise kannst du die Aufgaben schon recht gut lösen, aber oft machst du noch Fehler. Schau dir die Regeln noch einmal an und wiederhole die Übungen, bei denen du Probleme hattest.
0–18: Die Bedingungssätze bereiten dir noch große Probleme. Wiederhole die Regeln gründlich und mache die Übungen konzentriert noch einmal.



*Lösungen Seite 104*

# 3 Gerund, Infinitive and Participle Constructions

Jenny and Peter have joined their school's drama group recently. But that is not the only piece of news. In fact Jenny is going to take part in a dancing competition, Thomas is practising for a concert and Peter will be playing in a football match soon. All of them are quite excited about performing in front of a large crowd.

# 3.1 The Gerund

**Alles klar?!** ***Form and Functions of the Gerund***

Das **Gerundium** wird durch Anhängen von ***-ing*** an die Grundform des Verbs gebildet. Es ist eine Art substantiviertes Verb (vgl. im Deutschen „das Schwimmen", „beim Lesen") und besitzt sowohl Eigenschaften eines **Verbs** als auch Eigenschaften eines **Substantivs**. Die Wörter, nach denen es stehen kann, solltest du dir gut einprägen!

**Wie ein Substantiv kann es verwendet werden:**

- als Subjekt — ***Dancing*** *is fun.*
- als Objekt — *He likes* ***reading****.*
- nach einer Präposition — *She thanked him for* ***helping****.*
- als prädikative Ergänzung — *He is busy* ***learning****.*

**Wie ein Verb kann es verwendet werden:**

- mit direktem Objekt — *He loves* ***playing*** *the guitar.*
- mit adverbialer Bestimmung/Adverb — *She practised* ***dancing*** *happily.*

**Exercise 1** **Form sentences with a gerund as the subject.**

Jenny, Peter and their friends are talking about their hobbies:

| | | |
|---|---|---|
| swim | | healthy. |
| play football | | exhausting. |
| sing | | fun. |
| travel | is | expensive. |
| ski | | dangerous. |
| paint | | boring. |
| ride a horse | | difficult. |
| read | | interesting. |

1. ..........
2. ..........
3. ..........
4. ..........
5. ..........
6. ..........
7. ..........
8. ..........



*Lösungen Seite 104*

**Alles klar?!** ***The Gerund as an Object***

Nach einer Reihe von Verben steht im Englischen das Gerundium. Dazu gehören:

| | | | |
|---|---|---|---|
| *to admit doing sth.* | zugeben, etw. zu tun | *to include* | einschließen, beinhalten |
| *to avoid* | vermeiden | *to involve* | umfassen, beinhalten |
| *to consider* | in Betracht ziehen | *to keep* | weitermachen |
| *to dislike* | nicht mögen | *to mention* | erwähnen |
| *to enjoy* | genießen | *to mind* | etwas dagegen haben |
| *to escape* | entkommen | *to miss* | vermissen, verpassen |
| *to finish* | beenden | *to practise* | üben |
| *to give up* | aufgeben | *to quit* | aufgeben |
| *to hate* | hassen | *to risk* | riskieren |
| *to imagine* | sich vorstellen | *to suggest* | vorschlagen |

Vergleiche mit dem Deutschen:
*Anne enjoys* ***swimming*** *in the sea.* – etwa: Anne genießt das Schwimmen im Meer.

**Exercise 2** **Form sentences.**

1. Jenny – sometimes – enjoy – play – football – her brother Peter.

   ..............................................................................................

2. Why – Anne – avoid – meet – her German teacher?

   ..............................................................................................

3. Last week – her German teacher – consider – give – Anne – a bad mark.

   ..............................................................................................

4. Give up – smoke – Dad!

   ..............................................................................................

5. Mrs Wilson: "Job – involve – translate – interesting texts?"

   ..............................................................................................

6. Thomas – finish – practise – for the concert – soon.

   ..............................................................................................

7. "Thomas – you – ever – suggest – travel – to Canada – with your new girlfriend?"

   ..............................................................................................

8. Anne: "I – could not – imagine – be – an actress."

   ..............................................................................................

*Lösungen Seite 104*

## Alles klar?! *The Gerund after Prepositions*

a) Gerundium nach **Verben mit Präposition**:

*Jenny is looking forward to* **dancing** in the club.*
*She wants to prevent Peter from **telling** Richard that she fancies him.*

| | |
|---|---|
| *to accuse (so.) of doing sth.* | (jmdn.) anklagen wegen etw./..., etw. getan zu haben |
| *to agree with* | einverstanden sein mit |
| *to apologise for* | sich entschuldigen für |
| *to believe in* | glauben an |
| *to complain about* | sich beschweren über |
| *to decide for/against/between* | sich entscheiden für/gegen/zwischen |
| *to depend on* | abhängen von |
| *to dream of/about* | träumen von |
| *to feel like* | Lust haben auf |
| *to insist on* | bestehen auf |
| *to look forward to** | sich freuen auf |
| *to prevent (so.) from* | (jmdn.) abhalten von |
| *to succeed in* | Erfolg haben bei |
| *to talk about* | sprechen über |
| *to thank (so.) for* | (jmdm.) danken für |
| *to think of* | denken an |
| *to think about* | nachdenken über |
| *to worry about* | sich Sorgen machen wegen |

***Aufgepasst!**
Bei Verbindungen wie *to be/get used **to*** oder *to look forward **to*** ist ***to*** kein Teil des Infinitivs, sondern eine **Präposition**!

b) Gerundium nach Verbindungen von **Adjektiv und Präposition**:

*Thomas is excited about **giving** a concert.*
*He wants to be famous for **playing** the guitar.*

| | |
|---|---|
| *to be afraid of doing sth.* | Angst vor etw. haben/... davor haben, etw. zu tun |
| *to be angry about* | sich ärgern über |
| *to be bad/good at* | schlecht/gut sein in |
| *to be crazy about* | verrückt sein nach |
| *to be disappointed about* | enttäuscht sein über |
| *to be excited about* | aufgeregt ein wegen |
| *to be famous for* | berühmt sein für |
| *to be glad about* | froh sein über |
| *to be ideal for* | ideal sein für |
| *to be interested in* | sich interessieren für |
| *to be keen on* | versessen sein auf, sehr gern tun |
| *to be proud of* | stolz sein auf |
| *to be responsible for* | verantwortlich sein für |
| *to be sick of* | satt haben |
| *to be tired of* | es müde sein |
| *to be/get used to** | gewöhnt sein an/sich gewöhnen an |

c) Gerundium nach Verbindungen von **Nomen und Präposition**:

*Thomas has the choice between **studying** words and being lazy.*
*If he is lazy, he will be in danger of **failing** in the exam.*

| | |
|---|---|
| *advantage of* | Vorteil (von) |
| *choice between* | Wahl zwischen |
| *danger of* | Gefahr (zu) |
| *hope of* | Hoffnung (auf) |
| *(no/a faint) idea of* | (keine/eine vage) Vorstellung (von) |
| *interest in* | Interesse an |
| *opportunity of* | Gelegenheit (zu) |
| *possibility of* | Möglichkeit (zu) |
| *problem of* | Problem (zu) |
| *reason for* | Grund für |
| *risk of* | Risiko (zu) |

**Tipp!**
Versuche dir die Verbindungen mit Präpositionen und auch alle anderen Wörter und Konstruktionen, mit denen das Gerundium stehen kann, gut einzuprägen!

d) Außerdem folgt das Gerundium auf **allein stehende Präpositionen** und ist dann Teil einer **adverbialen Bestimmung**, z. B.

- der Zeit (nach *after*, *before*)
- des Grundes (nach *for*)
- der Art und Weise (nach *without*, *instead of*)
- des Mittels (nach *by*)
- der Einräumung (nach *in spite of*, *apart from*)

Im Deutschen kann die adverbiale Bestimmung auf unterschiedliche Weise wiedergegeben werden:

1. ***In spite of practising** a lot, Thomas cannot play this melody.*
   Obwohl Thomas viel übt, kann er diese Melodie nicht spielen. (Nebensatz)
2. *Anne left the youth club **without saying** goodbye.*
   Anne verließ den Jugendclub, ohne sich zu verabschieden. (Infinitivkonstruktion)
3. ***Before having** lunch, Mrs Wilson wants to go shopping.*
   Vor dem Mittagessen will Mrs Wilson einkaufen gehen. (Präposition und Nomen)

**Exercise 3** **Join the sentences using a gerund.**

1. Jenny is going to perform a modern dance tonight. She is excited about it.

   ..........................................................................................................................................

2. The Wilson family will have dinner first. After that they will all go and see Jenny dance.

   ..........................................................................................................................................

3. "Why are you so nervous? There is no reason for it."

   ..........................................................................................................................................

4. "I have never taken part in a dancing competition. I'm not used to it."

   ..........................................................................................................................................

5. Richard has also come to see her performance. He is glad about it.

   ..........................................................................................................................................

6. Jenny wins the competition! She is very proud of it.

   ..........................................................................................................................................

**Exercise 4** **Complete the sentences using gerunds and the correct prepositions.**

1. Anne insists .......... ................................ (go) to the club to tell everybody of Jenny's triumph.
2. Jenny is usually keen .......... ................................ (dance) in the disco. Today she even feels .......... ................................ (sing) for her friends.
3. Will I have the opportunity .......... ................................ (talk) to Richard at the club?
4. Thomas is looking forward .......... ................................ (play) at the concert next week; he is tired .......... ................................ (practise) every day.
5. Peter is not used .......... ................................ (play) as a goalkeeper. He is afraid .......... ................................ (lose) the next match.
6. The Wilsons are planning their holiday. They are thinking .......... ................................ (travel) to the USA. They have the choice .......... ................................ (drive) along the west coast on Highway 1 or ................................ (experience) the Indian Summer in New England in the east. Jenny is interested .......... ................................ (see) American skyscrapers.
7. Anne will be responsible .......... ................................ (feed) the cat when the Wilsons are on holiday. She will also have to think .......... ................................ (water) the plants.



*Lösungen Seite 105*

**Exercise 5** ★ **Replace the underlined parts of the sentences using a gerund. Choose from the expressions given below.**

*a reason for – to look forward to – to be happy about – to be bad at –*
*to feel like – to be keen on – to be famous for – to be good at*

1. Jenny and Anne absolutely want to go to Thomas's concert.

2. "Look over there! How wonderful to see that Richard is here, too!"

3. "Hi Jenny, congratulations! Everybody knows you because you dance now."

4. "Thank you! But I cannot play the guitar very well, whereas Thomas can play it so well."

5. Richard doesn't know why he shouldn't ask Jenny to go to the cinema with him.

6. "Would you like to watch the romantic comedy they are showing at the Odeon?"

7. "Yes, it will be great to watch that film next week!"

**Exercise 6** ★ **Form sentences using a gerund. Choose the correct preposition!**

1. After – win match – Peter's coach – thank him – defend – goal – so well.

2. "Mother – just – succeed – get – well-paid – new job!"

3. Peter – disappointed – not get – main part (= Hauptrolle) – school play.

4. Mr Wilson – accuse – Peter – use – his laptop to go online – without – ask.

5. Mrs Wilson – not agree – postpone – meeting.

*Lösungen Seite 105*

**Alles klar?!** ***The Gerund after Certain Phrases***

Das Gerundium steht auch nach folgenden festen Wendungen:
*It's no good/no use* ***thinking*** *about that now; it's too late.*

| | |
|---|---|
| *can't help* | einfach müssen |
| *how/what about* | wie wäre es mit |
| *it's no good* | es hat keinen Zweck |
| *it's no use* | es hat keinen Zweck |
| *it's (not) worth* | es lohnt sich (nicht) |

**Joke:**
*Mother kangaroo:*
*"It's raining again.*
*How about* ***playing*** *inside?"*

**Exercise 7** **Form sentences using gerunds. Insert prepositions where necessary.**

1. It was worth – go – Thomas's concert.

   ..........................................................................................

2. Jenny – can't help – think – Richard – all the time.

   ..........................................................................................

3. It's no use – deny – the boy who plays the main part – very good – act. (2 gerunds!)

   ..........................................................................................

4. Thomas – can't help – feel – anxious – about – grammar test – tomorrow.

   ..........................................................................................

5. It's no good – complain – not get – enough pocket money. (2 gerunds!)

   ..........................................................................................

6. How about – go out – for dinner – tonight?

   ..........................................................................................

*Lösungen Seite 105*

## 3.2 The to-Infinitive

**Alles klar?!** ***Form and Functions of the to-Infinitive***

Der Infinitiv ist die Grundform des Verbs. Wie das Gerundium hat er sowohl Eigenschaften eines **Verbs** als auch Eigenschaften eines **Substantivs**. Es hängt vom jeweiligen Verb, der Satzstruktur oder auch der Bedeutung ab, ob Infinitiv oder Gerundium steht. Präge dir deshalb die Wörterlisten in diesem Kapitel gut ein und bearbeite die Aufgaben gründlich!

**Wie ein Substantiv kann der Infinitiv mit *to* verwendet werden:**

- als Subjekt — ***To err*** *is human.*
- als Objekt — *Anne has decided* ***to leave****.*
- als prädikative Ergänzung — *Jenny's wish is* ***to join the dancing group****.*
- als adverbiale Bestimmung — *Thomas went to see his teacher* ***to talk to her.***
- als Attribut zu einem Nomen — *Jenny has a lot of work* ***to do****.*

**Wie ein Verb kann er verwendet werden:**

- mit einem Objekt — *Peter hopes* ***to get*** *a good mark.*
- mit Adverb/adverbialer Bestimmung — *Try* ***to plan*** *your presentation accurately.*

**Alles klar?!** ***The to-Infinitive as Object after Certain Verbs***

Nach einigen Verben steht im Englischen der Infinitiv mit *to*.

*We are planning* ***to go*** *swimming in the lake.* Dazu gehören:

| | | | |
|---|---|---|---|
| *to arrange to do sth.* | vereinbaren, etw. zu tun | *to plan* | planen |
| *to decide* | entscheiden | *to refuse* | sich weigern |
| *to expect* | erwarten | *to seem* | scheinen |
| *to hope* | hoffen | *to want* | wollen |
| *to learn* | lernen | *would like* | möchte(n) |

Nach einigen Verben kann ein Objekt gefolgt von *to* + Infinitiv stehen.

*Mrs Wilson expects Thomas* ***to work*** *hard for his exam.* Dazu gehören:

Verb → Objekt → to-Infinitiv

| | | | |
|---|---|---|---|
| *to advise so. to do sth.* | jmdm. raten, etw. zu tun | *to expect* | erwarten |
| *to allow* | erlauben | *to force* | zwingen |
| *to ask* | bitten | *to help* | helfen |
| | | *to invite* | einladen |
| | | *to teach* | lehren |
| | | *to tell* | sagen |
| | | *to want* | wollen |
| | | *to warn* | warnen |

**Aufgepasst!**
Anders als im Deutschen kann nach ***would like*** und ***want*** nie ein Nebensatz mit ***that*** („dass …") stehen!

**Exercise 1** **Form sentences.**

1. Jenny – hope – know – Richard – telephone number – by tomorrow.

   ..........................................................................................

2. Mr Wilson – expect – Thomas – pass – his A-level exams.

   ..........................................................................................

3. Yesterday – Mrs Wilson – tell – Jenny – not – get – new jacket – dirty.

   ..........................................................................................

4. Last Saturday – Peter – promise – be – home – before 11 pm.

   ..........................................................................................

5. Doctor – want – Mr Wilson – give up – smoking.

   ..........................................................................................

6. Mother – never – allow – Jenny – go – to the disco – next weekend.

   ..........................................................................................

7. We – decide – go on holiday – to Maine – and – watch – whales – next summer.

   ..........................................................................................

8. Jenny – you – would like – join – choir?

   ..........................................................................................

**Exercise 2** **Complete the text with infinitive constructions and suitable object pronouns where necessary. Use the given verbs.**

*take – practise – listen – speak – learn – work – decide – start – play – imagine – pay*

Jenny tells Thomas about the drama group: "At the beginning our teacher tells .................... .................... to his instructions. He wants .................................... together in pairs .................... .................... some dialogues. If there is a new play, he asks .................................... on which part we would like .................................... . Otherwise he expects .................................... rehearsing our current play. He always advises .................................... the characters we represent. Last week he warned .................................... (not) too fast. After one hour he allows .................................... a break. Afterwards he expects .................................... attention again. He is a great director! I hope .................................... a lot from him.



*Lösungen Seite 106*

**Alles klar?!** ***The to-Infinitive to Express a Purpose***

Der Infinitiv mit *to* kann für adverbiale Bestimmungen verwendet werden, die eine **Absicht** oder einen **Zweck** ausdrücken.

*This month Jenny is practising very often* ***(in order) to win*** *the competition.*
*You have to get up earlier* ***(in order) not to miss*** *the match.*

**Alles klar?!** ***The to-Infinitive after Adjectives and Nouns***

Der Infinitiv mit *to* steht auch **nach bestimmten Adjektiven** und **Substantiven**; er kann dann z. B. prädikative Ergänzung oder Attribut zu einem Nomen sein.

*Thomas thinks it is easy* ***to play*** *the guitar.*
*Jenny was surprised* ***to see*** *Richard at the concert.*
*Sometimes you need a friend* ***to talk*** *to.* (..., mit dem man reden kann.)
*We have a lot of grammar* ***to revise****.* (..., die wir wiederholen sollen.)

**Beachte!**
Hat der Infinitiv ein eigenes Subjekt, wird dieses mit ***for*** eingefügt:
*Was it difficult for Anne* ***to pass*** *the test?*
*There are many possibilities for you* ***to solve*** *that problem.*
Dies gilt auch bei Verben, die fest mit ***for*** verbunden sind:
*Anne waited for Jenny* ***to put*** *on her coat.*

**Alles klar?!** ***The to-Infinitive after Question Words and Certain Expressions***

Der Infinitiv mit *to* kann auch nach den Fragewörtern ***how, what, which, who, when, where*** und ***whether*** sowie nach ***the first, the last, the next*** und ***the only one/person*** stehen. Vorsicht: Diese Verwendung des Infinitivs unterscheidet sich sehr stark vom Deutschen!

*Peter is thinking about how* ***to ask*** *his father for some extra pocket money.*
*The Wilson family could not decide where* ***to go*** *on holiday.*
*Thomas was the last one* ***to hand*** *in his paper.*
*Peter is not the only pupil* ***to prefer*** *playing football to basketball.*

**Joke:**
*Mother: "What's going on in your room?"*
*Jenny: "Oh, that's just Grandpa explaining to Dad how* ***to do*** *my maths exercise."*

**Exercise 3** **Complete the sentences using infinitive constructions.**

1. Mrs Wilson has to go to the supermarket ... *(um Butter zu kaufen.)*

   ..........................................................................................

2. Why are you always ... *(der Letzte, der nach Hause kommt?)*

   ..........................................................................................

3. Tell me ... *(wann ich zu Hause sein soll.)*

   ..........................................................................................

4. Do you think ... *(es ist sehr schwer, Chinesisch zu lernen?)*

   ..........................................................................................

5. Thomas has told me ... *(wie ich zur neuen Bücherei komme.)*

   ..........................................................................................

6. It was not easy ... *(für Peter, die Rolle des verrückten Briefträgers zu akzeptieren.)*

   ..........................................................................................

7. Jenny is helping her parents ... *(um abends ausgehen zu dürfen.)*

   ..........................................................................................

8. What would be the best book ... *(das ich Anne schenken könnte?)*

   ..........................................................................................

**Exercise 4** **Replace the underlined parts of the sentences using infinitive constructions.**

1. Mr Wilson was angry <u>when he heard</u> that the price of petrol had risen again.

   ..........................................................................................

2. Richard would be foolish <u>if he did not invite</u> Jenny to the party.

   ..........................................................................................

3. Jenny was happy <u>that she had found</u> these jeans in the sales.

   ..........................................................................................

4. Is it a problem <u>if you have to come</u> earlier?

   ..........................................................................................

5. You will get a lot of exercises <u>that you can do</u> over the weekend.

   ..........................................................................................

6. Neil Armstrong was the first man <u>who walked</u> on the moon.

   ..........................................................................................



*Lösungen Seite 106*

## 3.3 Infinitive or Gerund?

**Alles klar?!** ***Infinitive and Gerund with a Difference in Meaning***

Bei einigen Verben **entscheidet** der nachfolgende Gebrauch von Infinitiv oder Gerundium über deren **Bedeutung**.
Zu diesen Verben gehören u. a.:

| | |
|---|---|
| • ***to remember/to forget*** **+ Infinitiv** | mit Bezug auf die **Zukunft**: |
| ***Remember to feed*** *the dog before you leave.* | – daran denken, etwas zu tun |
| *Don't* ***forget to switch*** *off the lights.* | – vergessen, etwas zu tun |
| • ***to remember/to forget + Gerundium*** | mit Bezug auf die **Vergangenheit**: |
| *Do you* ***remember feeding*** *that giraffe at the zoo last year?* | – sich daran erinnern, etwas getan zu haben |
| *I will never* ***forget meeting*** *him at the concert.* | – vergessen, etwas getan zu haben |
| • ***to stop/to go on*** **+ Infinitiv** | mit Bezug auf **neue Handlung**: |
| ***Stop to listen*** *to the teacher.* | – innehalten/anhalten, um etwas zu tun |
| *Then I* ***went on to explain*** *the problems.* | – als Nächstes etwas (anderes) tun |
| • ***to stop/to go on*** **+ Gerundium** | mit Bezug auf **bisherige Handlung**: |
| *You have to* ***stop complaining****.* | – aufhören, etwas zu tun |
| ***Go on running****.* | – weitermachen mit etwas |
| • ***to mean*** + **Infinitiv** | **Absicht**, etwas zu tun: |
| *I* ***meant to send*** *you a birthday card but I forgot.* | – wollen, vorhaben, beabsichtigen |
| • ***to mean*** **+ Gerundium** | logische **Folge** einer Sache: |
| *Being a successful football player* ***means training*** *hard almost every day.* | – bedeuten |
| • ***to try*** **+ Infinitiv** | Ausdruck des **Bemühens**: |
| *I* ***tried to translate*** *the sentence.* | – versuchen, etwas zu tun |
| • ***to try*** **+ Gerundium** | **Ausprobieren** einer Methode: |
| *If it doesn't work,* ***try using*** *the dictionary.* | – es versuchen mit etwas |

## Alles klar?! *Infinitive and Gerund with the Same Meaning*

Nach bestimmten Verben kann entweder der Infinitiv oder das Gerundium stehen, **ohne** dass es einen **Bedeutungsunterschied** gibt.
Zu diesen Verben gehören:

| | |
|---|---|
| *to begin doing/to do sth.* | anfangen, etw. zu tun |
| *to continue* | weitermachen |
| *to hate* | hassen |
| *to like* | mögen, gern machen |
| *to love* | lieben |
| *to prefer* | vorziehen |
| *to start* | beginnen |

## Exercise 1 Cross out the wrong verb form.

Peter: "Our teacher told us not to forget reading/to read Shakespeare's Macbeth over the Easter holidays."

Jenny: "Now I regret missing/to miss the play on TV last week. I stopped reading/to read after the scene in which the king is murdered, so I don't know the ending."

Peter: "So you must remember taking/to take the book with you on our trip. I'll try reminding/to remind you."

Jenny: "But that means reading/to read Shakespeare instead of having fun!"

Peter: "Well, then stop complaining/to complain and start reading/to read."

Jenny: "O.K. Although I prefer watching/to watch the play to reading/read it."

## Exercise 2 Match the fitting sentence parts.

| | |
|---|---|
| 1. Sorry, I don't remember | a) helping your mother in the kitchen? |
| 2. Don't forget | b) to drink a cup of coffee. |
| 3. Thomas is really good | c) to call me tomorrow. |
| 4. Jenny is interested | d) to go to the disco tonight. |
| 5. Would you mind | e) to make his father angry, so he apologised. |
| 6. Jenny is looking forward to | f) to close the windows. |
| 7. Please remember | g) at playing the guitar. |
| 8. Peter hadn't meant | h) talking to you. |
| 9. Jenny and Anne would like | i) meeting Richard again. |
| 10. Mr Wilson was tired, so he stopped | j) in listening to Richard's story. |



*Lösungen Seite 106/107*

**Exercise 3** ★ **Complete the sentences using either an infinitive or a gerund.**

1. Peter enjoys .............................. (play) football, whereas he hates .............................. (play) basketball.
2. What kind of music do you like .............................. (listen) to? – I love .............................. (listen) to classical music, which sometimes means .............................. (buy) expensive CDs.
3. You must stop .............................. (worry) about your problems and start .............................. (solve) them.
4. Do you know how .............................. (waltz)? – Mum tried .............................. (teach) me, but I am really bad at .............................. (dance). It's no use .............................. (try) again.
5. If you cannot win the match, try .............................. (develop) a new strategy!
6. Don't forget .............................. (take) this book back to the library. Do you remember .............................. (pay) the extra fee last month?
7. Thomas, are you interested in .............................. (paint)? – Sorry, but I prefer .............................. (play) the guitar to .............................. (paint).
8. Jenny and Peter are looking forward to .............................. (perform) a modern comedy next week.

*Lösungen Seite 107*

## 3.4 The Participle

**Alles klar?!** ***Form and Function of the Participle***

Beim **Partizip** unterscheidet man zwei Formen:
- Das ***present participle*** wird durch Anhängen der Endung ***-ing*** an den Infinitiv gebildet.
- Das ***past participle*** der regelmäßigen Verben besitzt die Endung ***-ed***, das der unregelmäßigen Verben muss extra gelernt werden – es steht in Verbtabellen in der dritten Spalte.

Das Partizip ist eine adjektivische Verbform und besitzt als solche sowohl Eigenschaften eines **Adjektivs** als auch Eigenschaften eines **Verbs**.

**Wie ein Verb kann es verwendet werden:**

| | |
|---|---|
| • mit einem Objekt | *Peter saw Jenny **reading** the book.* |
| • mit einer Konjunktion | *When **watching** TV, Peter heard that ManU had won.* |
| • in zusammengesetzten Zeitformen | *The girls are **dancing** at the moment.* |
| | ***Having read** the book, Jenny didn't watch the film.* |
| • im Passiv | ***Being questioned** by the teacher, Jenny became very nervous.* |

**Wie ein Adjektiv kann es z.B.:**

| | |
|---|---|
| • gesteigert werden | *The book was more **interesting** than she had expected.* |
| • mit Adverb verwendet werden | *The victory was absolutely **unexpected**.* |

**Wie ein Adjektiv** kann das Partizip außerdem **attributiv** gebraucht werden, d. h. ein Substantiv näher bestimmen. Dabei hat das *present participle* **aktive** Bedeutung, das *past participle* **passive** Bedeutung.

*Have you ever seen such a **boring** film?*
*Peter's **broken** leg hurt badly.*

Ebenso kann es **prädikativ** gebraucht werden, d. h. als Ergänzung zum Verb. Auch dabei muss die aktive und passive Bedeutung der beiden Formen unterschieden werden.

*I found this book **fascinating**.*
*Mrs Wilson looked **annoyed** when Jenny came home late.*

**Joke:**

*Teacher:* *"What are you painting, Peter?"*
*Peter:* *"Oh, that's a picture of a sheep **eating** grass."*
*Teacher:* *"But where's the grass?"*
*Peter:* *"The sheep has eaten it all."*
*Teacher:* *"And where's the sheep?"*
*Peter:* *"Well, **having eaten** all the grass, it went to another meadow."*

**Alles klar?!** ***The Participle instead of Certain Relative Clauses***

Besitzt ein Partizip eine Erweiterung, d. h. ein Objekt oder eine adverbiale Bestimmung, so steht das erweiterte Partizip **nach** dem Substantiv, auf das es sich bezieht.
Diese Konstruktion kann anstelle von **notwendigen Relativsätzen** stehen, in denen das **Relativpronomen Subjekt** ist. Dabei wird das *present participle* für einen Relativsatz im Aktiv verwendet, das *past participle* für einen Relativsatz im Passiv.

*The pupil* ***playing*** *the father is taller than Peter. (participle construction)*
*The pupil who plays the father is taller than Peter. (relative clause)*

*The play* ***written*** *by Goethe is difficult to perform. (participle construction)*
*The play which was written by Goethe is difficult to perform. (relative clause)*

**Exercise 1** ★ **Rewrite the sentences using participles instead of relative clauses.**

1. The people who are looking for me are my parents.

   ........................................................................................................

2. The person who is cutting your hair is doing a marvellous job!

   ........................................................................................................

3. The pizzas which are served at the new restaurant are great.

   ........................................................................................................

4. The woman who lives next door is my science teacher.

   ........................................................................................................

5. Science, the subject which she teaches (!), includes chemistry, biology and physics.

   ........................................................................................................

6. The example that is given below the text is difficult to understand.

   ........................................................................................................

7. The painter who was teaching here last year has gone to the south of France.

   ........................................................................................................

8. The man who is praising Peter for his excellent performance (= Leistung) is his football coach.

   ........................................................................................................

9. The car that Peter's friend Tim damaged yesterday has a broken mirror now.

   ........................................................................................................

*Lösungen Seite 107*

**Alles klar?!** ***The Participle instead of an Adverbial Clause***

Eine Partizipialkonstruktion kann, v. a. in der Schriftsprache, einen adverbialen Nebensatz ersetzen. Dabei steht das *present participle* für aktive, das *past participle* für passive Nebensätze.

- *When he was walking home, Peter saw the accident.* (Adverbialsatz der Zeit)
  ***Walking** home, Peter saw the accident.* (Partizipialkonstruktion)
- *As it was bought in the winter sales, this shirt cannot be returned.* (Adverbialsatz des Grundes)
  ***Bought** in the winter sales, this shirt cannot be returned.* (Partizipialkonstruktion)

Um eine Vorzeitigkeit im Nebensatz auszudrücken, wird die Konstruktion *having + past participle* für einen Aktivsatz, *having been + past participle* für einen Passivsatz verwendet.

- *As she had seen the film, Jenny knew the soundtrack.* (Adverbialsatz des Grundes)
  ***Having seen** the film, Jenny knew the soundtrack.* (Partizipialkonstruktion)

Ist der logische Zusammenhang des Satzgefüges nicht klar erkennbar, wird auch eine Partizipialkonstruktion mit einer entsprechenden Konjunktion eingeleitet.

- *Although **knowing** all the words, Thomas couldn't translate the text.*

**Exercise 2** **Replace the underlined adverbial clauses by participle constructions.**

1. While Thomas was translating the text, he had to look up several words in the dictionary.

   ..........................................................................................................

2. When Peter was asked to bring his favourite book, he chose *Harry Potter*.

   ..........................................................................................................

3. As they had finished their homework, Jenny and Anne went swimming.

   ..........................................................................................................

4. Mrs Wilson found Jenny's earring while she was cleaning the bathroom.

   ..........................................................................................................

5. When Jenny arrived home, she noticed that she had lost her key.

   ..........................................................................................................

6. As Mr Wilson was angry, he left his office.

   ..........................................................................................................

7. Although Peter expected the test, he didn't do his homework properly.

   ..........................................................................................................


*Lösungen Seite 108*

# 3.5 Infinitive or Participle?

**Alles klar?!** ***Infinitive and Participle after Verbs of Perception***

Nach **Verben der Wahrnehmung**, gefolgt von einem Objekt, kann im Englischen sowohl der Infinitiv (ohne *to*) als auch das Partizip Präsens stehen. Zu diesen Verben gehören:

| | | | |
|---|---|---|---|
| *to see so. doing/do sth.* | sehen, wie/dass jmd. etwas tut | *to hear* | hören |
| *to watch* | beobachten, an-/zuschauen | *to listen to* | an-/zuhören |
| *to notice* | bemerken | *to feel* | fühlen |
| | | *to smell* | riechen |

Das **Partizip Präsens** wird verwendet, wenn das Geschehen noch nicht beendet, sondern im Ablauf begriffen ist, und deshalb nur ein „Ausschnitt" davon wahrgenommen wird.

*I saw Jenny **talking** to her teacher* (... wie Jenny gerade mit ihrem Lehrer sprach.)

Den **Infinitiv** verwendet man, wenn das Geschehen vollständig wahrgenommen wird. Dies betrifft meistens sehr kurze, „punktuelle" Handlungen.

*I saw Jenny **enter** her classroom.* (... wie/dass Jenny das Klassenzimmer betrat.)

**Exercise** **Complete the sentences using a present participle or an infinitive.**

Mrs Wilson tells her husband what she saw, heard and smelt while she was walking their dog Rex:

"When I closed the door, I heard our neighbour, Mr Patel, .............................. (sing) in the bathroom. At the same time, I saw his wife .............................. (leave) the house, .............................. (get) into her car and .............................. (drive) off in a hurry. Further down the street I heard Mrs Wright, the opera singer, .............................. (practise), when I saw her son .............................. (kiss) his girlfriend behind a tree. .............................. (cross) the main street, I could hear several people .............................. (argue). Then I saw someone .............................. (slam) the front door and .............................. (run) away. Only a few minutes later I noticed a police car .............................. (approach). I felt my heart .............................. (beat) faster. I watched the policemen .............................. (enter) the house. But soon everything became quiet again. So I could continue my walk with Rex. .............................. (arrive) at the park at last, Rex was happy smelling all the other dogs .............................. (run) around, and I enjoyed listening to the birds .............................. (chirp) in the trees."

*Lösungen Seite 108*

## Test your Progress (40 minutes)

**Exercise 1** **Choose the correct verb form, either infinitive or gerund, and the correct preposition, where necessary.**

1. Inviting Richard to the party means ................................ (introduce) him to all your friends.
2. It's no good ................................ (stay) up all night if you have to get up in the morning.
3. Anne was the only one ................................ (think) the latest *James Bond* film was boring.
4. Did you enjoy ................................ (spend) the weekend in the mountains?
5. Thomas finally succeeded ................................ (be invited) to perform at the Cavern Club.
6. His friend Daniel wants Peter ................................ (visit) him in Munich next summer.
7. Do you find it difficult ................................ (learn) German, Jenny?
8. Thank you ................................ (walk) the dog!

Points: [ ] out of 10

**Exercise 2** **Put the verbs into their correct form.**

1. Mrs Wilson likes ...................... (read) detective stories, so why not ...................... (give) her an Agatha Christie novel as a present?
2. Have you ever watched Dad ...................... (try) ...................... (play) ice hockey?
3. Jenny, you must remember ...................... (remind) Anne that she will be responsible for ...................... (feed) the cat next weekend.
4. Listen to Jenny ...................... (sing)! She hopes ...................... (win) the song contest.
5. We can begin ...................... (eat) without ...................... (wait) for Dad; he will be late today.
6. You must avoid ...................... (get) into a traffic jam because we are invited ...................... (join) the party at our neighbours'.
7. Richard, would you like ...................... (come) to my birthday party? Don't worry about how ...................... (get) home, my father will take you.
8. I could see you ...................... (smoke). It's no use ...................... (lie).
9. ...................... (play) football is great, especially after ...................... (be) at school till 3 pm.

Points: [ ] out of 18


*Lösungen Seite 108/109*

**Exercise 3** **Replace the underlined clauses using participle constructions.**

1. After the girls had closed the door behind them, they sat down to talk.

   ..........................................................................................

2. While Jenny was listening to her favourite singer, she tried to do her maths homework.

   ..........................................................................................

3. Thomas went to the travel agency because he had been told to fetch some catalogues.

   ..........................................................................................

4. Although Peter was treated fairly by his German teacher, he didn't like her.

   ..........................................................................................

5. Thomas happily accepted the holiday job which was offered to him.

   ..........................................................................................

6. Mr Wilson went to the delicatessen because he wanted to prepare a special dinner.

   ..........................................................................................

7. After he had spent all his pocket money, Peter asked Thomas to lend him £ 10.

   ..........................................................................................

Points: ☐ out of 7

**Exercise 4** **Fill in the correct verb forms.**

Thomas is introducing his new girlfriend to his parents:

"This is Lisa from Cardiff. In her free time she likes .............................. (play) the drums in her band and sometimes enjoys .............................. (read) historical novels. Lisa's sister teaches her how .............................. (take) really beautiful photos with her digital camera. Lisa doesn't mind .............................. (help) her little brother with his homework. She is keen on .............................. (go) to clubs, but rarely during the week because she can't stand .............................. (be) too tired to get up the next morning. She has decided .............................. (study) medicine after her A-levels and wants .............................. (become) a surgeon. She dreams of .............................. (travel) to foreign countries and even considers .............................. (work) abroad for a couple of years as a doctor."

Points: ☐ out of 10

*Lösungen Seite 109*

**Exercise 5** **Find the mistakes and correct them. There is one mistake in each sentence.**

1. Our football coach has considered to introduce new rules.

   ..............................................................................................................

2. Jenny is used to sing at the youth club.

   ..............................................................................................................

3. The doctor told you to stop to smoke.

   ..............................................................................................................

4. The new book writing by John Grisham is a bestseller again.

   ..............................................................................................................

5. I heard the door bell ringing three times, so I knew it was Jenny.

   ..............................................................................................................

6. Mrs Wilson wants that Thomas lays the table today.

   ..............................................................................................................

7. Are you also looking forward to spend your holidays in New England in the USA?

   ..............................................................................................................

8. Please remember feeding the dog tomorrow.

   ..............................................................................................................

9. Peter was disappointed about not to win the match.

   ..............................................................................................................

Points: ☐ out of 9

Total points: ☐ out of 54

49–54: Super! Du beherrschst die Konstruktionen mit Gerundium, Infinitiv und Partizip sehr gut!

26–48: Teilweise kannst du die Aufgaben schon recht gut lösen, aber oft machst du noch Fehler. Schau dir die Regeln noch einmal an und wiederhole die Übungen, bei denen du Probleme hattest.

0–26: Die Konstruktionen mit Gerundium, Infinitiv und Partizip bereiten dir noch große Probleme. Wiederhole die Regeln gründlich und mache die Übungen konzentriert noch einmal.



*Lösungen Seite 109*

4

# Nouns and Articles

So far, Jenny, Peter and Thomas have done really well. But now they can't wait for their holidays to come, and there is still so much work to do for school. At least, the Wilson family are making plans for their summer trip. They are all travelling to the east coast of the United States. As the USA is quite a long way away, the Wilsons will have to go there by plane. All of them are looking forward to this big adventure.

## 4.1 Singular and Plural

**Alles klar?!** ***Countable and Uncountable Nouns***

**Zählbare** Nomen sind solche, die im **Singular einen Vertreter** ihrer Gattung benennen und **im Plural mehrere**. Sie können nicht nur mit dem bestimmten Artikel, sondern auch **mit Zahlwörtern und dem unbestimmten Artikel** verwendet werden.

- *five books*
- *two trees*
- *an idea*

**Unzählbare** Nomen – wie etwa *milk, tea, land* – bezeichnen meist Stoffliches oder Kategorien, die keine Identifikation einzelner Vertreter zulassen. Sie haben **keinen Plural** und können **weder mit dem unbestimmten Artikel noch mit Zahlwörtern** verwendet werden. Um hier eine Menge von Elementen zu bezeichnen, muss eine „Hilfskonstruktion" mit einem Begriff verwendet werden, der diese Nomen zählbar macht.

- *(ten bottles of) milk*
- *(five cups of) tea*
- *(a piece of) land*

**Tipp:**
Manche Nomen werden sowohl zählbar als auch unzählbar verwendet, allerdings oft mit einem Bedeutungsunterschied! Ein Beispiel ist *hair*. Als unzählbares Nomen bezeichnet es „alle Haare": *What colour **is your hair**?* Sind dagegen einzelne, „zählbare" Haare gemeint, kannst du den Plural bilden: *Look, there **is a hair/are two hairs** in my soup!*

**Sammelbegriffe** und **abstrakte Begriffe** sind im Englischen in der Regel **nicht zählbar**. Sie besitzen dann **keinen Plural** und werden mit **Verben und Pronomen im Singular** verwendet. Um sie zählbar zu machen, kann man die **Umschreibung *"a piece of ..."*** verwenden.
Zu diesen Begriffen gehören u. a.:

**Sammelbegriffe:**

| | |
|---|---|
| *furniture* | Möbel, Mobiliar |
| *equipment* | Ausrüstung |
| *homework* | Hausaufgabe(n) |

**abstrakte Begriffe:**

| | |
|---|---|
| *advice* | Rat, Ratschläge |
| *damage* | Schaden, Schäden |
| *information* | Information(en) |
| *knowledge* | Wissen, Kenntnis(se) |

*Peter wrote down all the **information** he could find.* (... alle Informationen ...)
*The new **piece of furniture** in Thomas's room **was**n't cheap.* (Das neue Möbel[stück] ...)

Daneben gibt es im Englischen eine Reihe von Nomen, die trotz ihrer **Pluralendung auf *-s*** wie ein **Nomen im Singular** verwendet werden, z. B.:

| | | | |
|---|---|---|---|
| *math(ematic)s* | Mathematik | *dominoes* | Domino |
| *news* | Nachrichten | *darts* | Darts |
| *physics* | Physik | *billiards* | Billard |
| *politics* | Politik | *measles* | Masern |
| *the United States* | die Vereinigten Staaten | *mumps* | Mumps |

***Physics*** *is very interesting.*
***Darts*** *is very popular in Great Britain.*

**Exercise 1** **Add a suitable expression.**

Today Peter has to do the shopping for his mother. Complete the shopping list using the following expressions:

*half a pound of – two bottles of – one bar of – five – a packet of – one kilo of – one*

.......................................... apples

.......................................... milk

.......................................... flour

.......................................... chicken

.......................................... washing powder

.......................................... butter

.......................................... chocolate

**Exercise 2** **Choose the correct version.**

1. Have you got a/any homework today?
2. The United States is/are bigger than Germany.
3. Our weekend trip was terrible because we had awful/an awful weather and the furniture in our hotel room was/were very old and run down.
4. Mum, can you help me? I need an/some advice.
5. Listen to the news. – What is it/are they about?
6. Peter, your hairs look/hair looks terrific!
7. Measles is/are quite a serious illness for old people.

*Lösungen Seite 109/110*

## Alles klar?! Plural Nouns

Im Englischen gibt es Nomen, die **nur im Plural verwendet** werden. Diese können nicht mit dem unbestimmten Artikel verwendet werden. Die entsprechenden Verben und Pronomen müssen ebenfalls im Plural stehen. Zu dieser Gruppe von Nomen gehören:

| | |
|---|---|
| *clothes* | Kleidung |
| *stairs* | Treppe(nhaus) |
| *thanks* | Dank |
| *wages* | (Monats-)Lohn, Löhne |

*Those **clothes** are quite expensive.*

Zu dieser Gruppe zählen auch die **Paarwörter *(pair nouns)***, welche Dinge bezeichnen, die aus zwei Teilen bestehen. Zur Bezeichnung einer genaueren Menge wird der Ausdruck *„a pair of …“ bzw. „two/three/… pairs of …“* verwendet. Dazu zählen u. a.:

| | |
|---|---|
| *jeans* | Jeans |
| *leggings* | Leggings |
| *pants (AE)* | (lange) Hose |
| *pyjamas* | Schlafanzug |
| *shorts* | kurze Hose |
| *swimming trunks* | Badehose |
| *trousers* | (lange) Hose |
| *glasses* | Brille |
| *headphones* | Kopfhörer |
| *scissors* | Schere |

*Are these **trousers** new?*
*I've bought two pairs of **shorts**.*

**Eselsbrücke:**
Engländer haben zwei Beine und sind stolz darauf! Deshalb legen sie großen Wert auf den Plural bei Beinkleidern wie *trousers, shorts, leggings, …*

## Exercise 3 Complete the list.

Peter is going on a 5-day football camp. List what he puts into his suitcase.

.............................................. T-shirts

.............................................. shorts

.............................................. jeans

.............................................. sweaters

.............................................. pyjamas

.............................................. socks

.............................................. tracksuit

*Lösungen Seite 110*

**Alles klar?!** ***Collective Nouns***

Eine weitere Besonderheit sind Substantive, die eine **Gruppe von Menschen** bezeichnen: Wenn man die **Gruppe als Einheit** sieht, stehen im Englischen das Verb und die entsprechenden Pronomen im **Singular**. Wenn dagegen die **einzelnen Mitglieder der Gruppe** gemeint sind, stehen Verb und Pronomen im Plural.
Solche Gruppenbezeichnungen sind u. a.:

| | |
|---|---|
| *army* | Armee |
| *audience* | Publikum |
| *band* | Band |
| *class* | Klasse |
| *club* | Verein, Club |
| *couple* | Paar |
| *crew* | Besatzung |
| *crowd* | Menschenmenge |
| *enemy* | Feind |
| *family* | Familie |
| *government* | Regierung |
| *group* | Gruppe |
| *majority* | Mehrheit |
| *management* | Geschäftsleitung |
| *party* | Partei |
| *press* | Presse |
| *public* | Öffentlichkeit |
| *staff* | Personal, Kollegium |
| *team* | Mannschaft, Team |

*Peter's football* ***team*** *is winning the match.*
*His* ***team*** *are discussing their new strategy.*

***Class*** *8b is complete now.*
*The* ***class*** *take out their exercise books.*

Es gibt jedoch auch **Gruppenbezeichnungen**, die **nur** mit dem **Plural** verwendet werden können; dazu gehören u. a.:

| | |
|---|---|
| *cattle* | Vieh |
| *people* | Leute |
| *police* | Polizei |

*The* ***police*** *are questioning the witnesses.*

**Exercise 4** **Form sentences from the words given below.**

1. The Wilson family – discuss – holiday plans – for three hours – now

   ..............................................................................................................

2. Dad – worried – wages – decrease – since last June

   ..............................................................................................................

3. Audience – very interested – journalists' presentation

   ..............................................................................................................

4. Management – my firm – announce – results – of the tests – tomorrow

   ..............................................................................................................

5. Jenny – think – youth club – be – great fun

   ..............................................................................................................

6. Jenny – black leggings – be – too small

   ..............................................................................................................

7. Peter – need – three new – shorts

   ..............................................................................................................

8. This – be – second – jeans – you – bought – this week

   ..............................................................................................................

9. Who – know – where – scissors – be? And – where – be – my glasses?

   ..............................................................................................................

*Lösungen Seite 110*

## 4.2 Definite and Indefinite Article

**Alles klar?!** ***The Definite Article***

Den bestimmten Artikel verwendet man, wenn das darauffolgende Substantiv näher bestimmt ist. Für **abstrakte Substantive**, **Stoffbezeichnungen** und **Zeitangaben** gilt im Unterschied zum Deutschen: Sie stehen **ohne Artikel**, wenn sie **allgemein verwendet** und nicht näher bestimmt werden. Werden sie jedoch – z. B. durch einen Relativsatz oder einen mit *of* verbundenen Zusatz – **näher bestimmt**, dann stehen sie **mit dem bestimmten Artikel**.
Zu diesen Begriffen gehören:

- abstrakte Substantive wie *history, life, nature, society, progress*
- Stoffbezeichnungen wie *bread, food, water*
- Zeitangaben (Monate, Wochentage, Feiertage, Mahlzeiten) wie *February, Monday, Christmas, breakfast*

*Jenny thinks that **life** isn't always easy.*
*She is fascinated by **the life** of Cleopatra in ancient Egypt.*
*Dad won't be home for **dinner** today.*
*Did you like **the dinner** we had the other day?*

**Beachte:** In Verbindung mit *next* und *last* entfällt bei Zeitangaben der bestimmte Artikel.

***Next July** Thomas is going to travel to Canada.*

**Öffentliche Einrichtungen** wie *church, hospital, school* oder *prison* werden im Englischen
- **mit** dem **bestimmten Artikel** gebraucht, wenn das **Gebäude** gemeint ist, und
- **ohne Artikel** verwendet, wenn der **Zweck** der Einrichtung im Vordergrund steht.

*Mrs Wilson had to go to **hospital** for an operation.*
*Her husband went to **the hospital** to see her.*

**Eigennamen**
- der meisten Seen, Bergen, Straßen, Gebäuden stehen im Englischen in der Regel **ohne den bestimmten Artikel**, ebenso Personennamen, denen ein Adjektiv vorausgeht.
- von Flüssen und Meeren, Museen, Theatern und Hotels sowie Eigen- und Familiennamen im Plural werden in der Regel **mit dem bestimmten Artikel** verwendet.

*Lizzie lives on **Kingston Road**.*
*Look at **poor Ben**!*
***The Danube** is a big river in the south of Germany.*
*I love hiking in **the Alps**.*
*I have invited **the Millers** for dinner.*

Anders als im Deutschen wird im Englischen der **bestimmte Artikel** bei *all, both, double, half, most of* und *twice* **nachgestellt**.

*He will have read **half the** book by Thursday.*
*What did you do **all the** time?*

Als feststehende Wendung wird im Englischen die Verbindung von ***play*** **+ Musikinstrument** immer mit bestimmtem Artikel verwendet.

*Thomas plays **the guitar**.*

**Exercise 1** **Fill in the definite article where necessary.**

*Jenny:* I'm so tired. I don't want to go to ......... school today.

*Mrs Wilson:* Well, it's already ......... Friday! So take a shower and eat ......... breakfast I've prepared for you, and you will survive!

*Jenny:* But I don't feel like ......... cereal and ......... milk today.

*Mrs Wilson:* Take it or leave it, but hurry up! I don't want you to be late for ......... history again.

Jenny: Oh, we will only talk about ......... society of the Middle Ages.

*Mrs Wilson:* Isn't it interesting what ......... life was like then?

*Jenny:* Well, I would prefer sleeping and dreaming of my own life.

**Joke:**
*"My son spent six years at university taking **medicine**." – "Oh dear! Is he well now?"*



***Lösungen Seite 110***

**Alles klar?!** ***The Indefinite Article***

Der unbestimmte Artikel wird verwendet, wenn das darauffolgende Substantiv nicht näher bestimmt ist. Anders als im Deutschen werden **Personenbezeichnungen**, die z. B. die **Zugehörigkeit zu einer Religion, Nationalität oder Berufsgruppe** ausdrücken, normalerweise **mit dem unbestimmten Artikel** verwendet.

*Peter wants to become* ***a*** *football player.*
*Is your friend* ***a*** *Buddhist?*

**Vor Zeit- und Maßangaben** steht der unbestimmte Artikel in der Bedeutung **„pro"/„je"**.

*Football training takes place three times* ***a*** *week.*
*Tomatoes are £ 2,–* ***a*** *pound.*

Im Unterschied zum Deutschen steht der unbestimmte Artikel in vielen Fällen auch nach *as* („als") und *without* („ohne").

*Don't leave home without* ***an*** *umbrella.*
*Use that book as* ***a*** *writing pad.*
(Aber Vorsicht: *They left without permission/without delay.)*

Anders als im Deutschen wird im Englischen der unbestimmte Artikel bei *half, quite, rather, such* und *what* **nachgestellt**.

*What* ***a*** *mess!*
*It will take me half* ***a*** *day to clean it.*

Im Englischen gibt es eine Reihe von **Redewendungen** mit dem unbestimmten Artikel. Dazu gehören:

| | |
|---|---|
| *(to be) in a hurry* | in Eile (sein) |
| *have (got) a cold/a headache/a temperature* | eine Erkältung/Kopfweh/Fieber haben |
| *to have/take a bath/a shower* | baden/duschen |
| *to take a seat* | Platz nehmen |
| *an hour and a half, one and a half hours* | eineinhalb Stunden |
| *for a long time* | (für) lange Zeit/seit langer Zeit |
| *It is a pity!/What a pity!* | (Wie) schade! |

**Exercise 2** ★ **Complete the sentences translating the German parts in brackets.**

1. Staying at the Hilton costs £ 110 ........................................................ *(pro Nacht).*
2. Anne always talks of ........................................................ *(Lehrerin zu werden).*
3. During her holidays, Jenny is going to work ........................................................ *(als Kellnerin).*
4. Mr Wilson cannot go to work because ........................................................ *(er Kopfweh hat).*
5. *(Ihr habt eineinhalb Stunden)* ........................................................ to write the essay.
6. Are you going to ........................................................ *(heute Abend baden)*?
7. *(Man braucht eine halbe Stunde)* ........................................................ to get to the city centre.
8. You are not allowed to drive a car ........................................................ *(ohne Führerschein).*

**Exercise 3** **Complete the sentences using the definite or indefinite article where necessary.**

1. Could I have ......... glass of ......... water?
2. ......... women do not always use ......... make-up.
3. Do you like ......... make-up I bought yesterday?
4. ......... children love ......... Christmas.
5. What ......... good essay that is!
6. Are you going to ......... church ......... next Sunday?
7. I've never been to ......... British Museum.
8. Your colleague is ......... Hindu, isn't he? What does he eat for ......... lunch?
9. Have you ever visited ......... Millers on ......... Green Street?
10. Did you know the performance would be without ......... break?

*Lösungen Seite 111*

## Test your Progress (20 minutes)

**Exercise 1** **Fill in the correct forms of the verbs and pronouns.**

1. Mrs Wilson: "Peter, are you going to wear .............................. (this/these) jeans today? .............................. (It/They) .............................. (need) washing soon."
2. We are going on a field trip today. Our class .............................. (meet) at the station.
3. Our teacher says physics .............................. (be) easier to understand outdoors. But all the equipment .............................. (have) to be carried along.
4. Don't forget the scissors. We'll need .............................. (the scissors).
5. .............................. (be) your team complete? The second group .............................. (leave) in ten minutes.
6. People .............................. (not want) to be disturbed!
7. Oh dear, I forgot my sunglasses! Now the sun is shining, so I need .............................. (my sunglasses).
8. If I had taken along my swimming trunks, I could have worn .............................. (my swimming trunks) for a swim in that nice lake.
9. When we got back to our school, the police .............................. (ask) questions. .............................. (the police) .............................. (look) for witnesses to an accident.
10. Our homework .............................. (be) to fill in this worksheet.

Points: [ ] out of 16

**Exercise 2** **Fill in the definite or indefinite article where necessary.**

1. Are you feeling better? Can you go to ......... school tomorrow?
2. Have you tried ......... bread from the new bakery?
3. My favourite subject is ......... biology.
4. I have to go to ......... hospital to show Anne her homework.
5. We usually meet at ......... Piccadilly Circus before we go to the cinema.
6. Did you know that Tim plays ......... trumpet?
7. Mary's father is ......... doctor.

Lösungen Seite 111/112

8. I can't concentrate because I have ......... headache again.
9. Today we had to write an essay about ......... pollution.
10. Do you know anything about ......... history of the Middle Ages?

Points: ☐ out of 10

**Exercise 3** **Find the mistakes and correct them.**

1. I was so tired yesterday. I only saw the half film.
2. You must not enter the room without permission of the boss.
3. Have you seen my red leggings? I can't find it.
4. I need more informations about holiday jobs.
5. When you come to London, you must visit the Buckingham Palace.
6. I have spent all my pocket money on two sunglasses.
7. Thomas, you must not be late three times the week.
8. Have you got a homework today?
9. The United States are very important for Germany's export industry.
10. Peter is player in the local football team.

Points: ☐ out of 10

Total points: ☐ out of 36

33–36: Super! Du beherrschst den Gebrauch der Artikel und die Verwendung von Singular- und Pluralformen schon sehr gut!

18–32: Teilweise kannst du die Aufgaben schon recht gut lösen, aber oft machst du noch Fehler. Schau dir die Regeln noch einmal an und wiederhole die Übungen, bei denen du Probleme hattest.

0–17: Die richtige Verwendung von Singular- und Pluralformen sowie der Gebrauch der Artikel bereiten dir noch große Probleme. Wiederhole die Regeln gründlich und mache die Übungen konzentriert noch einmal.


*Lösungen Seite 112*

5

# Adverbs as Adverbials

Being very optimistic, Mrs Wilson has taken part in a prize competition run by a big Italian food company. Surprisingly, she has won the first prize, which is a one-week holiday in Rome, including non-stop flights, accommodation, delicious meals, sightseeing tours and quite a lot of entrance fees – for the whole family! Having read the letter, Mrs Wilson phones her husband immediately to tell him the good news.
And when Jenny, Peter and Thomas arrive at home, they all get very excited about their holiday in Italy.

## 5.1 Kinds of Adverbs

**Alles klar?!** ***Adverbs of Manner, Place, Time and Frequency***

Diese Arten von Adverbien kennst du wahrscheinlich schon:

- Adverbien der **Art und Weise** wie *fantastically, quickly, intelligently, exactly*
  *Thomas is driving **slowly**.*
- Adverbien des **Ortes** wie *here, (over) there, everywhere*
  *Mrs Wilson buys her clothes **there**.*
- Adverbien der **Zeit** wie *today, yesterday, now, then*
  *The weather will be fine **tomorrow**.*
- Adverbien der **Häufigkeit** wie *never, sometimes, often, usually, always*
  *Peter **usually** plays football after his homework.*

**Aufgepasst!**
Das **Adverb** ist eine **Wortart**! Wenn ein einzelnes Adverb als vollständiges **Satzglied** fungiert, nennt man dieses ***adverbial (of time, place etc.)*** bzw. – auf Deutsch – **adverbiale Bestimmung (der Zeit, des Ortes etc.)**. Es gibt auch *adverbials*, die aus anderen Wortarten (*every day, to Edinburgh, ...*), mehreren Adverbien *(very often, extremely rarely)* oder sogar aus Nebensätzen *(... when I was a boy, ... because he liked it)*, Infinitiv-, Gerund- oder Partizipialkonstruktionen *(to reach this aim ..., after setting the table ..., although planning for a long time ...)* bestehen.

**Alles klar?!** ***Adverbs of Degree and Comment***

**Gradadverbien** beziehen sich auf ein anderes Adverb, ein Adjektiv oder ein Verb und schwächen dieses ab oder verstärken es.

*Peter's latest English test was **very** good.*
*Jenny could **hardly** concentrate because of the noise.*

Dazu gehören u. a.:

| | | | |
|---|---|---|---|
| *a bit* | ein bisschen | *pretty* | ziemlich |
| *absolutely* | völlig | *quite* | ganz, ziemlich |
| *a lot* | viel | *rather* | ziemlich |
| *at all* | überhaupt | *really* | wirklich |
| *completely* | ganz | *scarcely* | kaum |
| *hardly* | kaum | *very (much)* | sehr |

**Kommentierende Adverbien** geben die Haltung des Sprechers zum Inhalt des Satzes wieder. Zu dieser Gruppe von Adverbien gehören z. B.:

| | |
|---|---|
| *actually* | tatsächlich |
| *apparently* | scheinbar |
| *fortunately* | glücklicherweise |
| *hopefully* | hoffentlich |
| *obviously* | offensichtlich |
| *of course* | natürlich |
| *probably* | wahrscheinlich |
| *unfortunately* | leider |

***Fortunately**, the flight to Rome was on time.*
*We don't have to visit all the sights on the first day, **of course**!*

**Exercise** **Underline the adverbs in the following text and write them into the appropriate columns. Can you also find adverbials made up from more than one word?**

After having landed at Rome International Airport, the Wilsons are confidently looking for their transfer bus to the hotel. On their way through Rome they are amazed about the unexpectedly bustling traffic. "Luckily, I do not have to drive here. I have never seen such traffic chaos! Rome is an extraordinarily lively city," Mr Wilson admits.

As the bus is pretty crowded, they are really glad to arrive at their hotel. The entrance hall is elegant and brightly lit. A friendly young man receives them cordially at the reception desk and congratulates Mrs Wilson with a bottle of champagne, then he hands the room keys over to her.

While they are waiting for the lift to the fifth floor, Jenny is watching all the well-dressed people surrounding them. Peter isn't absolutely sure whether the man just entering the hall is the famous Italian football star Luca Toni. And Thomas is apparently attracted to the group of beautiful Italian girls standing over there and chatting cheerfully.

What a brilliant start into a promising Italian holiday!

| manner | place/direction | time/frequency | degree | comment |
|---|---|---|---|---|
| | | | | |

*Lösungen Seite 112*

## 5.2 Position of Adverbials

**Alles klar?!** ***General Rules for the Position of Adverbials***

| ***Front-Position*** ***Adverb(s) or Phrase*** | ***Subject (+ Auxiliary)*** | ***Mid-Position*** ***Adverb(s) or Phrase*** |
|---|---|---|
| | *Alex* | *sometimes ...* |
| *However,* | *we don't* | *always ...* |
| *Unfortunately,* | *the vegetables are* | *sometimes ...* |
| adverbials of comment | | adverbials of indefinite time |
| .................................... | | .................................... |
| .................................... | | .................................... |
| | | adverbials of indefinite frequency |
| | | .................................... |
| | | .................................... |

**Aufgepasst!**
Als Vollverb steht ***to be*** immer vor dem Adverb mit *mid-position.*
(Haupt-)Verb und Objekt dürfen nie getrennt werden.
Adverbien der bestimmten Zeit und des Ortes können in ***front-position*** stehen, wenn sie besonders betont sind.

**Alles klar?!** ***Position of Adverbs of Degree***

Gradadverbien als **Attribute** (d. h. als Teil eines Satzglieds) stehen normalerweise vor dem Wort, das sie verstärken oder abschwächen.
*Mrs Wilson was **absolutely** surprised.*

Einige Gradadverbien, die als **adverbiale Bestimmung** (d. h. als vollwertiges Satzglied) im Satz stehen wie *a bit, a lot, at all* oder *very much*, stehen meist in *end-position.*
*Do you know Rome **at all**?*
*Thank you **very much**.*



*Lösungen Seite 113*

**Exercise 1** **Write examples of the different kinds of adverbials into the empty lines.**

| ***Main Verb (+ Object)*** | ***End-Position*** ***Adverb(s) or Phrase*** |
|---|---|
| *... cooks* | *on Fridays.* |
| *... like his meals.* | |
| *... burnt* | *nowadays.* |
| | adverbials of manner |
| | .................................................... |
| | adverbials of place |
| | .................................................... |
| | adverbials of definite time |
| | .................................................... |
| | adverbials of definite frequency |
| | .................................................... |

**Beachte!**
Kommen zwei adverbiale Bestimmungen der gleichen Art vor, so steht die genauere vor der weniger genauen. (Beispiel: *They met at a bar in Munich (place) at 8 o'clock today* (time).

**Eselsbrücke:**
Die Reihenfolge der Adverbialen der **Art und Weise**, des **Ortes** und der **Zeit** entspricht der alphabetischen Reihenfolge ihrer Anfangsbuchstaben: ***manner*** → ***place*** → ***time***

**Exercise 2** **Mark the correct position of the adverb in the sentence.**

1. I wear special clothes for my job. *sometimes*
2. I work at weekends. *often*
3. I work with my hands. *usually*
4. My job is creative. *really*
5. I work outdoors. *often*
6. I work with animals. *hardly*
7. You have to be strong. *in fact*
8. You do not need a university degree. *at all*

What kind of job could be described here? Have a guess!

*Lösungen Seite 113*

**Exercise 3** **Form sentences matching the phrases and write them down in your exercise book.**

| | | | |
|---|---|---|---|
| Mr and Mrs Wilson | often | go to a musical | in London. |
| Jenny | always | liked pizza | before. |
| Thomas | soon | has been to Italy | on Fridays. |
| I | sometimes | eat fish | at the Vatican. |
| You | rarely | listened to classical music | ten years ago. |
| Mr Wilson | never | will see the Swiss Guard | when he was a child. |

**Exercise 4** ★ **Form sentences from the words given.**

1. Mr Wilson – speak – not very well – Italian – unfortunately

   ..................................................................................................................

2. The Wilsons' guide – Marco – live – in Rome – for twenty years – happily

   ..................................................................................................................

3. Jenny – like – Italian ice-cream – very much

   ..................................................................................................................

4. Mrs Wilson – a delicious Italian cappuccino – sometimes – makes – for herself

   ..................................................................................................................

5. Thomas – unfortunately – be – late – for the sightseeing tour

   ..................................................................................................................

6. you – hopefully – enjoy – meals – at our restaurant

   ..................................................................................................................

7. the Wilsons – in the evening – unfortunately – have to – walk – upstairs – because – lift – not work – properly

   ..................................................................................................................

   ..................................................................................................................

8. Peter – apparently – too much – eat – prepared – deliciously – pasta

   ..................................................................................................................



*Lösungen Seite 113/114*

## Test your Progress (20 minutes)

**Exercise 1** **Put the adverbs into their correct position.**

1. Jenny was allowed to go to the disco next to the hotel with Thomas (yesterday – in fact).

   ..................................................................................................................................

2. There were a lot of young Italian people (actually – there).

   ..................................................................................................................................

3. They met some nice people, who could also speak English (fortunately – there).

   ..................................................................................................................................

4. It was funny when Thomas tried to talk to a pretty girl in Italian (however – really).

   ..................................................................................................................................

5. The music was not too loud, so they had to shout (not at all – luckily).

   ..................................................................................................................................

6. Jenny danced a lot (quite – of course).

   ..................................................................................................................................

7. Thomas liked the modern Italian music that was played (especially – before midnight).

   ..................................................................................................................................

8. Jenny and Thomas would like to go again (there – on Saturday – really).

   ..................................................................................................................................

Points: [ ] out of 17

**Joke:**

*Mrs Wilson: "Why are you writing so* ***slowly****?"*
*Peter: "Oh, it's a postcard for Tim's little brother, and he can't read very* ***quickly****."*

*Lösungen Seite 114*

**Exercise 2** **Find the mistakes and correct them.**

1. Mr Wilson locked carefully their safe and left the room.
2. The chambermaid changes the bedclothes always on Saturdays and Wednesdays.
3. Crossing the street in front of their hotel, Mrs Wilson had almost an accident.
4. "Dad, have you been ever to Rome?"
5. They have decided already to take the guided tour through the *Forum Romanum*.
6. "Mum and Dad, we'll see you at eight o'clock at the restaurant."
7. "We must now really leave!"
8. Peter obviously is looking forward to visiting the Colosseum.

Points: ☐ out of 8

Total points: ☐ out of 25

22–25: Super! Du beherrschst die Verwendung von Adverbien und adverbialen Bestimmungen schon sehr gut!

13–21: Teilweise kannst du die Aufgaben schon recht gut lösen, aber oft machst du noch Fehler. Schau dir die Regeln noch einmal an und wiederhole die Übungen, bei denen du Probleme hattest.

0–12: Die richtige Verwendung von Adverbien und adverbialen Bestimmungen bereitet dir noch große Probleme. Wiederhole die Regeln gründlich und mache die Übungen konzentriert noch einmal.

 *Lösungen Seite 114*

6

# Vocabulary

Every year before Easter the Wilson family work together to spring-clean their house. This year they are additionally planning the renovation of the attic to convert it into a new and bigger room for Peter. So there is a lot to do, and next week there will be a long weekend – ideal to put their plans into action!

## 6.1 Phrasal Verbs

**Alles klar?!** ***Formation***

*Phrasal verbs* bestehen aus einer Verbindung von **Verb + Adverb**, deren Bedeutung sich meist nicht von den Einzelbestandteilen ableiten lässt und die man daher als neue Wortschatzeinheit lernen muss. Dabei ist das Adverb eng mit dem Verb verbunden und darf nicht ohne Weiteres davon getrennt werden.

Die folgende Liste enthält eine Auswahl häufig verwendeter *phrasal verbs* mit ihren wichtigsten Bedeutungen. Vervollständige sie mithilfe von *Exercise 1*.

| ***Phrasal Verb*** | ***Meaning*** | ***Translation*** |
|---|---|---|
| *break .........* | when a car stops going | .................................................. |
| *break in* | 1. .............................................. | 1. einbrechen |
| | 2. .............................................. | 2. *(neue Schuhe)* einlaufen |
| *break .........* | discontinue | abbrechen |
| *bring up* | raise | .................................................. |
| *calm down* | become quiet | .................................................. |
| *carry .........* | continue | weitermachen |
| *carry out* | perform | .................................................. |
| *clear up* | tidy up: Please clear up this mess! | .................................................. |
| *drop off* | Could you drop me off at the hotel? | .................................................. |
| *fill in* | .................................................. | *(Formular)* ausfüllen |
| *find out* | .................................................. | herausfinden |
| *get .........* | .................................................. | entkommen |
| *get back* | return | .................................................. |
| *get .........* | leave (a vehicle) | .................................................. |
| *get .........* | 1. .............................................. | 1. (in ein Fahrzeug) einsteigen |
| | 2. continue | 2. weitermachen |
| *get up* | rise: I got up at 9 am today. | .................................................. |
| *give .........* | 1. give as a present | 1. ver-/herschenken |
| | 2. reveal *(a secret)* | 2. .............................................. |
| *give .........* | surrender: Do not give ..... to him! | nachgeben |
| *give up* | 1. surrender: Are you giving up? | aufgeben, ........................ |
| | 2. stop *(doing sth.)* | (etw.) aufgeben, ........................ |
| *go ahead* | .................................................. | weitermachen |
| *go on* | 1. continue: Go on with it! | 1. .............................................. |
| | 2. happen: What's going on here? | 2. .............................................. |
| *grow up* | .................................................. | aufwachsen |
| *hang .........* | wait | warten |



*Lösungen Seite 114/115*

| ***Phrasal Verb*** | ***Meaning*** | ***Translation*** |
|---|---|---|
| *leave out* | ................................................ | aus-/weglassen |
| *look after* | Kate is looking after little Jim tonight. | ................................................ |
| *look .........* | search (for) | suchen |
| *look out* | ................................................ | aufpassen |
| *look .........* | ................................................ | nachschlagen |
| *make up* | ................................................ | erfinden |
| *put .........* | delay, postpone | ................................................ |
| *put .........* | What dress should I put ..... tonight? | anziehen |
| *put up* | put up a cupboard/a building | ................................................ |
| *ring .........* | hang up | (Hörer) auflegen |
| *run away* | leave suddenly | ................................................ |
| *run .........* | get empty | leer werden |
| *run out (of)* | to run out of peas/peas have run out | ................................................ |
| *set off* | leave, get on one's way | ................................................ |
| *speak .........* | speak louder | lauter sprechen |
| *take .........* | 1. remove *(clothes)* | 1. *(Kleidung)* ausziehen |
| | 2. leave the ground | 2. abheben *(Flugzeug)* |
| *throw away* | ................................................ | wegwerfen |
| *try on* | put on to see if it fits | ................................................ |
| *turn .........* | 1. lower the volume | 1. leiser stellen |
| | 2. reject: Why did he turn ..... this offer? | 2. ................................................ |
| *turn .........* | 1. change direction | 1. abbiegen |
| | 2. press a button to stop sth. | 2. ausschalten |
| *turn up* | 1. appear: He turned up late last night. | 1. ................................................ |
| | 2. increase the volume | 2. ................................................ |
| *wake up* | 1. arouse so. from sleeping | 1. ................................................ |
| | 2. ................................................ | 2. aufwachen |
| *work .........* | calculate | herausfinden, errechnen |
| *write .........* | make a note | aufschreiben, notieren |

**Exercise 1** **Complete the table above with the following words and phrases.**

**Adverbs (can occur more than once!):** away – down – for – in – off – on – out – up

**Synonyms and explanations:** become an adult – check in a book – commit burglary – complete – continue – discover – enter (a vehicle) – escape – get rid of – invent – omit – stop sleeping – watch out, pay attention – wear new shoes until they are comfortable

**Translations:** ablehnen – *(jmdn. mit dem Auto)* absetzen – anprobieren – aufbrechen – aufhören mit – *(z. B. auf Kinder)* aufpassen – aufräumen – aufstehen – aufstellen, errichten – auftauchen – aufwecken – *(Kinder)* aufziehen – (aus einem Fahrzeug) aussteigen – durch-/ausführen – eine Panne haben – fast keine ... mehr haben/ausgehen – geschehen – kapitulieren – lauter stellen – preisgeben, verraten – sich beruhigen – (auf später) verschieben – weglaufen – weitermachen – zurückkehren

*Lösungen Seite 114/115*

**Exercise 2** **Complete the sentences using a suitable phrasal verb from the list on pages 64 and 65. Mind the tenses.**

1. Mr Wilson will be late for dinner because his car .......................................
2. Everything is very dusty in the attic. Don't forget to ....................................... old clothes.
3. Peter must ....................................... the costs for his new furniture.
4. The drilling machine is too loud, I can't hear you. .......................................!
5. The electric screwdriver doesn't work. The batteries .......................................
6. Jenny, you've been talking on the phone for half an hour. ....................................... now and start helping us!
7. If the paint doesn't dry till tomorrow, we must ....................................... our further plans.
8. I'm not ready yet. ....................................... a minute.
9. What's that noise? What ....................................... in the living room?
10. After getting the missing tools from the hardware store, Thomas can ....................................................... (you) at the youth club.

**Joke:**

*Why was Cinderella **thrown out** of the football team?*
*Because she **ran away** from the ball.*

 *Lösungen Seite 115*

**Alles klar?!** ***Word Order***

Es gibt sowohl *phrasal verbs*, die transitiv (= mit Objekt) verwendet werden, als auch solche, die intransitiv (= ohne Objekt) sind.
Bei **transitiven** *phrasal verbs* entscheidet die Art des Objekts über seine Stellung im Satz.

Ist das Objekt

- ein Nomen, so kann es vor oder nach dem Adverb stehen.
  *Peter's coach decided to* ***put*** *the match* ***off*** *for another week.*
  *Mrs Wilson* ***took off*** *her coat and* ***turned on*** *the radio.*
- ein Pronomen, muss es vor dem Adverb stehen.
  *Thomas was sleeping, so his mother didn't* ***wake*** *him* ***up****.*
- sehr lang, so steht es meist nach dem Adverb.
  *Jenny had to* ***look up*** *several words and their spelling.*

**Exercise 3** **Complete the sentences by translating the German parts into English.**

1. I have to go and get some more wooden boards; ... *(macht mit eurer Arbeit weiter, während ich weg bin.)*

   ........................................................................................................................

2. Peter and Thomas are arguing and ... *(keiner der beiden will nachgeben.)*

   ........................................................................................................................

3. Have you seen Rex? ... *(Ich habe ihn schon überall gesucht.)*

   ........................................................................................................................

4. Read the instructions properly and then ... *(führe sie aus.)*

   ........................................................................................................................

5. When Jenny was late for work yesterday, ... *(versuchte sie eine Ausrede zu erfinden).*

   ........................................................................................................................

6. Can you please help me ... *(diesen Schrank aufzustellen)?*

   ........................................................................................................................

*Lösungen Seite 116*

## 6.2 Collocations

**Alles klar?!** ***Definition***

Eine **Kollokation** ist eine Verbindung von Wörtern, die häufig gemeinsam auftreten. Normalerweise handelt es sich dabei um verschiedene Wortarten, wie z. B. Adjektiv + Nomen oder Verb + Nomen.

Im Folgenden lernst du einige wichtige *collocations* kennen, die du dir gut einprägen solltest, um häufige Fehler zu vermeiden!

> **Lerntipp:** Wie bei allen Vokabeln wird dir auch das Lernen von *collocations* und ihrer Bedeutung leichter fallen, wenn du dir die Wortverbindungen in Gruppen merkst. Du kannst sie z. B. in Wortfelder und Wortfamilien zusammenfassen oder mehrere Kollokationen lernen, die mit einem bestimmten Wort gebildet werden.

**Exercise 1** **Collocations with "make" and "do"**

**Fill the empty lines with the German equivalent of each collocation.**
**If you are not sure about some of them, look them up in a dictionary.**

**make**

... a coffee

..............................................

... friends

..............................................

... a decision

..............................................

... a mess

..............................................

... money

..............................................

... a cake

..............................................

... a mistake

..............................................

... a phone call

..............................................

... a good impression

..............................................

... an appointment

..............................................

... the bed

..............................................

... up your mind

..............................................



*Lösungen Seite 116*

**do**

... your homework

..............................................

... the washing-up

..............................................

... nothing

..............................................

... damage

..............................................

... the cleaning

..............................................

... the shopping

..............................................

... (something) for a living

..............................................

... the cooking

..............................................

... the ironing

..............................................

... your best

..............................................

... someone a favour

..............................................

... well

..............................................

**Exercise 2** **Translate the expressions in brackets into English. Mind the tenses!**

1. The Wilsons ...................................................... *(haben die Entscheidung getroffen)* that Peter may move into the attic room.
2. Peter has to look for a holiday job ...................................................... *(um Geld zu verdienen)* for his new furniture.
3. *(Kannst du mir einen Gefallen tun)* ...................................................... and prepare some sandwiches, Jenny?
4. I'm going to clean the windows ...................................................... *(nachdem ich meine Hausaufgaben gemacht habe).*
5. Thomas, ...................................................... *(kannst du die Einkäufe machen)* today?
6. *(Ich habe einen Termin vereinbart)* ...................................................... with an architect for tomorrow to ask him if we can tear down this wall.
7. Peter, if you ...................................................... *(gut abschneidest)* in your next maths test, we will pay for you new furniture.
8. Thomas ...................................................... *(hat schon Freundschaft geschlossen)* with the owner of the do-it-yourself store.

*Lösungen Seite 116*

**Exercise 3** ★ **Collocations with food and drink**

**Match each word in the first column with one in the second and write the complete expression into the empty line next to it.**

| | | |
|---|---|---|
| tap | potatoes | ........................................................ |
| scrambled | water | ........................................................ |
| roast | salad | ........................................................ |
| sparkling | beef | ........................................................ |
| fruit | coffee | ........................................................ |
| herbal | beans | ........................................................ |
| mashed | eggs | ........................................................ |
| baked | water | ........................................................ |
| white | tea | ........................................................ |

**Exercise 4** ★ **Football collocations**

**Fill the words given below into the empty lines to form football collocations, and put their German translation in the brackets.**

*score – hit – qualify – take – fail – commit – take – deflect – make – blow*

1. ...................................... the whistle (= ........................................................)
2. ...................................... for the championship (= ........................................................)
3. ...................................... a shot (= ........................................................)
4. ...................................... to score (= ........................................................)
5. ...................................... a goal (= ........................................................)
6. ...................................... the lead (= ........................................................)
7. ...................................... a foul (= ........................................................)
8. ...................................... a substitution (= ........................................................)
9. ...................................... the post (= ........................................................)
10. ...................................... a free kick (= ........................................................)



*Lösungen Seite 117*

**Exercise 5** **Complete the text using correct forms of the verbs given in exercise 4.**

Last weekend Peter's favourite football team, Chelsea, had an important match to ........................................ for the next championship. Only four minutes after the referee ........................................ the whistle, the new striker ........................................ a goal and his team ........................................ the lead. But then one of the defenders ........................................ a foul outside the penalty area, so the other team ........................................ a free kick. Luckily, the ball ........................................ the post! Although their coach ........................................ two substitutions, they didn't ........................................ a goal. And when the referee ........................................ the final whistle, Peter was happy with his team winning!

**Exercise 6** ★ **Computer collocations**

**With which of the nouns given below do the following verbs form a collocation? Some verbs may occur in more than one list.**

*crash – get – open – reply to – check – shut down – play on – delete – reboot – send – receive – create – back up*

| **... the computer** | **... a (computer) file** | **... an e-mail** |
|---|---|---|
| .................................................. | .................................................. | .................................................. |
| .................................................. | .................................................. | .................................................. |
| .................................................. | .................................................. | .................................................. |
| .................................................. | .................................................. | .................................................. |
| .................................................. | .................................................. | .................................................. |
| .................................................. | .................................................. | .................................................. |

## 6.3 Idioms

**Alles klar?!** ***Definition***

Bei einem ***idiom*** handelt es sich um einen feststehenden Ausdruck, der aus mehreren Wörtern besteht und dessen Bedeutung nicht aus den Einzelbedeutungen seiner Bestandteile zu erschließen ist. **Idiomatische Wendungen** sind feste Verbindungen, die kaum Veränderungen zulassen und als sprachliche Einheit gelernt und verwendet werden müssen.

**Exercise 1** ★ **Idioms from the area of food and drink**
**Match each idiom on the left with the correct explanation on the right.**

| | |
|---|---|
| to be like chalk and cheese | to be fantastic |
| something makes your mouth water | to love eating sweet things |
| not for all the tea in China | to have good results |
| to have a sweet tooth | to be completely different |
| to bear fruit | an important and powerful person |
| a big cheese | something makes you want to eat it |
| to be the best/greatest thing since sliced bread | not even for a great reward |

**Exercise 2** ★ **Idioms connected with animals**
**Complete the idioms given below with the following nouns, which are similar in German.**

*lion – fly – fox – butterflies – bee – wolf – peacock – dogs – chicken*

1. Mr Lang, our neighbour, never goes out to meet people; he is **a lone** ........................ .
2. Anne's cousin Jill is **as busy as a** ........................ and **as sly as a** ........................ .
3. Having done most of the work by himself, Peter is **as proud as a** ........................ .
4. You don't have to be afraid of Mr Lang. He **wouldn't hurt a** ........................ .
5. The new owner isn't able to run that business. I'm afraid it will **go to the** ........................ .
6. After the alarm they were all in a panic and **running round like headless** ........................**s**.
7. The workers didn't get much of the profit because the management took **the** ........................**'s share**.
8. Jenny was so nervous, she **had** ........................ **in her stomach** when she met Richard.

**Lerntipp:** Wenn du idiomatische Wendungen in deine persönliche Vokabelliste aufnimmst, notiere sie dir mit einem typischen Anwendungsbeispiel.



*Lösungen Seite 118*

**Exercise 3** ★ **Idioms related to houses**

**Complete the idioms with the correct alternative. Use a dictionary if necessary.**

1. Jenny and Anne are very good friends. They **get on like a** .....
   a) house on fire b) burning house c) fire in the house
2. Thomas **hit the** .... when Peter told him that he had broken his bike.
   a) wall b) roof c) floor
3. Jenny, why don't you listen to me. **It's like talking to a** .....
   a) wooden door b) metal fence c) brick wall
4. Peter wanted to build a balcony, but without enough money, his plan **went out of the** .....
   a) chimney b) window c) door
5. This terrible noise of the drilling machine **is driving me** ......
   a) up the stairs b) out of the house c) up the wall
6. Mr Wilson **smokes like a** ...... He must give up smoking.
   a) fireplace b) cooker c) chimney

**Exercise 4** ★ **Mixed idioms**

**Translate the expressions printed in bold, using German idioms with the same meaning.**

1. This wall painting will be **the icing on the cake** in your new room, Peter!

   ..............................................................................................................

2. If you buy the wooden boards on your way home, you can **kill two birds with one stone**.

   ..............................................................................................................

3. Cleaning the windows is **not** really **my cup of tea**.

   ..............................................................................................................

4. It was just a minor mistake, so don't **make a mountain out of a molehill**!

   ..............................................................................................................

5. When Mrs Wilson is talking to his teachers, Peter would like to **be a fly on the wall**.

   ..............................................................................................................

6. Anne's new hockey coach is even worse than the one before. The team got **out of the frying pan into the fire**. ..............................................................................

7. Jenny **acts as a guinea pig** in an experiment for a school project.

   ..............................................................................................................

**Lerntipp:** Wenn du dir bei einem *idiom* nicht sicher bist, schlag im **Wörterbuch** nach. Mit einer CD-Rom wird es dir nicht schwerfallen, den Ausdruck zu finden. Falls du aber mit einem gedruckten Buch arbeitest, solltest du wissen, unter welchem Stichwort du das *idiom* findest. Lies dir dazu am besten die Benutzerhinweise am Anfang durch.

*Lösungen Seite 118/119*

## 6.4 False Friends

**Alles klar?!** ***Definition***

Bei sogenannten ***false friends*** handelt es sich um Wörter, die im Deutschen und Englischen ähnlich aussehen, deren Bedeutung jedoch unterschiedlich ist. Aufgrund ihrer äußeren Ähnlichkeit werden diese vermeintlich leicht zu erschließenden Wörter jedoch oft falsch verwendet oder übersetzt. Daher solltest du dir die richtige Bedeutung bzw. Entsprechung besonders gut einprägen. Es folgt eine Liste häufiger *false friends* mit ihrer jeweils richtigen Übersetzung im Deutschen und Englischen sowie Beispielen zur Anwendung:

**aktuell ≠ *actual***
- aktuell = *current*
  *What is your current problem?*
- *actual* = tatsächlich
  *The actual value of this painting is higher.*

**bekommen ≠ *become***
- bekommen = *get, have, receive*
  *Peter got a bike for his birthday.*
- *become* = werden
  *Jenny wants to become a dancer.*

**brav ≠ *brave***
- brav = *good*
  *Tim has always been a good boy.*
- *brave* = mutig
  *James Bond is very brave.*

**Chips ≠ *chips***
- Chips = *crisps (BE), potato chips (AE)*
  *Jenny ate a packet of crisps in the cinema.*
- *chips (BE)* = Pommes Frites
  *Fish and chips for me, please!*

**dezent ≠ *decent***
- dezent = *discreet*
  *She is wearing discreet clothes today.*
- *decent* = anständig
  *Sophie turned out to be a decent girl.*

**engagiert ≠ *engaged***
- engagiert (einsatzfreudig) = *committed*
  *Jenny is a committed dancer.*
- *engaged* = verlobt
  *Mr and Mrs Wilson had been engaged for one year before they got married.*

**eventuell ≠ *eventually***
- eventuell = *maybe, perhaps*
  *Perhaps he will come to the party.*
- *eventually* = schließlich
  *Eventually Mrs Wilson allowed Jenny to go out.*

**finden ≠ *find***
- finden (i. S. v. denken) = *think, like*
  *I think we should rather go home now.*
  *How do you like this painting?*
  *I think it is pretty ugly.*
- *find* = (auf-)finden, entdecken
  *I can't find my keys!*

**Gift ≠ *gift***
- Gift = *poison*
  *This poison is very dangerous.*
- *gift* = Geschenk
  *This picture was a great gift.*

**Gymnasium ≠ *gymnasium***
- Gymnasium = *grammar school*
  *Does he go to grammar school yet?*
- *gymnasium* = Turnhalle
  *In winter our football training takes place in the gymnasium.*

**Handy ≠ *handy***
- Handy = *mobile phone*
  *I got a new mobile phone for my birthday.*
- *handy* = praktisch
  *This electric screwdriver is really handy.*

**Mappe ≠ *map***
- Mappe = *folder, briefcase*
  *Put your worksheet into the green folder.*
- *map* = Landkarte
  *Can you find Sidney and Melbourne on this map of Australia?*

**Menü ≠ *menu***
- Menü = *set meal*
  *What is the second course of this set meal?*
- *menu* = Speisekarte
  *Mrs Wilson is looking at the menu.*

**Rente ≠ *rent***
- Rente = *pension*
  *Tim's grandma gets a pension of £ 2,000 a month.*
- *rent* = Miete
  *The rent for the house has risen by £ 100.*

**See ≠ *sea***
- (der) See = *lake*
  *Have you ever been to the Great Lakes on the border between Canada and the USA?*
- *sea* = Meer („die See")
  *The Dead Sea is famous for its salty water.*

**sensibel ≠ *sensible***
- sensibel = *sensitive*
  *Jill's so sensitive, she starts crying easily.*
- *sensible* = vernünftig
  *Don't waste your money, be sensible!*

**Exercise** **Translate the words in brackets.**

1. Don't be afraid. Our dog Rex won't hurt you; he is always .................................... (= brav).
2. I can't .................................... (= finden) Thomas! – How do you .................................... (= findest) him? – I .................................... (= finde) he has become a .................................... (= anständiger) young man.
3. Have you heard the .................................... (= aktuellen) weather forecast?
4. He doesn't get enough .................................... (= Rente) to pay his .................................... (= Miete).
5. Old people can be very .................................... (= sensibel).
6. Could I .................................... (= bekommen) a glass of white wine, please?
7. Let's have a look at the .................................... (= Landkarte) before we get lost.
8. Have you always been such a .................................... (= engagierter) football player?
9. Our .................................... (= Gymnasium) has a big new .................................... (= Turnhalle).
10. I'll give you my .................................... (= Handy) if you want to call him.

*Lösungen Seite 119*

## Test your Progress (30 minutes)

**Exercise 1** **Complete the sentences with appropriate verbs.**

1. I can't hear anything. Can you .............................. the music up a bit?
2. Unfortunately Richard had to .............................. off his party until next month.
3. My grandpa is almost deaf, so you really have to .............................. up!
4. Finally, Mr Wilson will .............................. up smoking.
5. I can't believe her. I think she .............................. the whole thing up.
6. Hiking in these new shoes wasn't a good idea. I should have .............................. them in.
7. Babysitting isn't an easy job if you have to .............................. after three little children.
8. Can you .............................. me off at the library on your way to the office?
9. Don't tell your little brother, or he'll .............................. away our secret again.
10. He got a great offer, so why did he .............................. it down?

Points: ☐ out of 10

**Exercise 2** **Choose the correct alternative.**

1. Have you made/met a decision?
2. My computer doesn't work properly. I have to delete/reboot it.
3. Peter's team took/overtook the lead.
4. The coach had to do/make two substitutions.
5. You got all the points in your test. Well done/made!
6. I'd like a cup of white/milk coffee.
7. Unfortunately, the ball has beaten/hit the post.
8. This e-mail might contain a virus, so you had better shut it down/delete it.
9. Have you made/done all your homework?
10. They made up/made friends 30 years ago.

Points: ☐ out of 10



*Lösungen Seite 119*

**Exercise 3** **Complete the sentences using idioms instead of the parts in brackets.**

1. On my birthday I am having a pool party with cocktails, and these artificial palm trees will be ........................................................................ *(an extra that makes it perfect)*!
2. When Jenny told her mother that she had taken her new necklace, Mrs Wilson almost ........................................................................ *(burst with anger)*.
3. I would never do a bungee-jump, ........................................................................ *(not even for a lot of money)*.
4. I have underestimated Mr Miller. He is ........................................................................ *(very cunning)*.
5. Our old English teacher, Mrs Peters, was very strict, but with Mr Black we got ........................................................................ *(into an even worse situation)*.
6. If you are talking about your problem all the time, you ........................................................................ *(are exaggerating it)*.
7. For Thomas a car of his own would be ........................................................................ *(absolutely fantastic)*.
8. With the new chef you can hardly eat at that restaurant any more. I'm sure it will ........................................................................ *(have to close)*.
9. This kind of modern art isn't really ........................................................................ *(what I like)*.
10. You have worked hard, and eventually your efforts will ........................................................................ *(have good results)*.

Points: ☐ out of 10

*Lösungen Seite 120*

**Exercise 4** **Fill in the correct word.**

1. This is a(n) ................................... report dealing with the financial crisis.
   a) actual b) current c) present

2. Yesterday he gave me that lovely ring. Now we are ................................... .
   a) committed b) engaged c) united

3. If you want to keep on living here, you have to pay your ................................... on time.
   a) pension b) rent c) salary

4. Anne's mum is pregnant. She is going to ................................... a baby.
   a) become b) receive c) have

5. What do you ................................... is the right decision?
   a) mean b) say c) think

6. My skin is very ................................... . I have to be careful.
   a) sensible b) sensitive c) senseless

7. ................................... I'll come for a short visit, but I'm not sure yet.
   a) Eventually b) Possibly c) Anyway

8. Listen, if you are ................................... and tidy up your room, you will get some ice-cream afterwards.
   a) broken b) brave c) good

Points: ☐ out of 8

Total points: ☐ out of 38

34–38: Super! Du beherrschst die Anwendung dieser schwierigen Wortschatzeinheiten schon sehr gut!

19–33: Teilweise kannst du mit schwierigerem Wortschatz schon recht gut umgehen, aber oft machst du noch Fehler. Schau dir das Kapitel noch einmal an und wiederhole die Abschnitte, bei denen du Probleme hattest.

0–18: Die richtige Anwendung von etwas schwierigerem Wortschatz bereitet dir noch große Probleme. Wiederhole dieses Kapitel gründlich und mache die Übungen konzentriert noch einmal.

**Tipp:** Wenn du dir den Wortschatz in diesem Kapitel gut einprägst, kannst du damit in der Schule glänzen und deinen Lehrer beeindrucken. Und wenn du die gelernten Ausdrücke bei Klassenarbeiten richtig anwendest, wirst du im Bereich „sprachliche Ausdrucksfähigkeit“ richtig punkten und so deine Note verbessern!



*Lösungen Seite 120*

7

# Listening and Reading Comprehension – American English

Jenny and Peter's class are working on a project about the United States of America. Each pupil has had to choose a topic related to the USA and prepare an interesting presentation. There will be an exhibition in the school on July 4$^{th}$, Independence Day. Whereas Jenny is busy collecting information on national parks, Peter is learning a lot about native Americans.

## 7.1 American Indians

Searching the internet for information on American Indians, Peter has found an audio podcast entitled "Wounded Knee".

**Alles klar?!** ***Listening Comprehension***

Das **Hörverstehen** ist eine komplexe Fertigkeit, die richtig Spaß machen kann! Du solltest dir jedoch bewusst sein, dass du nicht jedes einzelne Wort erfassen musst, um die wesentlichen Inhalte eines Hörtexts zu begreifen. Denke daran, dass es unterschiedliche Arten des Zuhörens und verschiedene Aufgabenstellungen gibt:

- Manchmal geht es nur darum, die wesentlichen Inhalte zu verstehen *(listening for gist)*.
- Wenn die Aufgabe jedoch auf bestimmte Informationen und Details abzielt, musst du den Text genau auf diese Informationen hin anhören *(listening for detail)*. Dazu kannst du dir schon während des Anhörens stichpunktartig Notizen machen.
- Es gibt auch Aufgaben, bei denen du konkret einzelne Wörter oder Wortgruppen heraushören und in Lücken einsetzen musst. Wenn du dabei ein Wort nicht eindeutig verstehst, achte beim Einsetzen darauf, dass das Wort, das du in die Lücke schreibst, sowohl inhaltlich als auch grammatikalisch in den Satz passt.

**Tipp zum Hörverstehen:** Lies dir immer zuallererst die gestellte Aufgabe genau durch, damit du weißt, worauf du beim Zuhören besonders achten musst!

**Exercise 1** **Go to www.gute-noten-in.de/lernen/en/8/audio and listen to the audio "Wounded Knee". Then tick the correct answer. (If you haven't got internet – but only then! –, you can use the text on page 82 as a reading comprehension text.)**

| **Wounded Knee** | **true** | **false** | **not in text** |
|---|---|---|---|
| 1. The Indian Removal Act said that the American Indians had to sell their land. | | | |
| 2. In 1876, all Native Americans were sent to reservations. | | | |
| 3. The Native Americans didn't want European food because they hadn't known it before. | | | |
| 4. In their reservations the Native Americans couldn't find enough animals for hunting. | | | |
| 5. The "Ghost Dance" was a war dance. | | | |
| 6. The US government sent soldiers because they were afraid of an attack by the Native Americans. | | | |
| 7. Wounded Knee was an Indian leader in South Dakota. | | | |
| 8. Within five minutes, about three hundred American Indians were killed by soldiers. | | | |
| 9. The Native Americans stopped their protest after the massacre. | | | |


*Lösungen Seite 120/121*

**Exercise 2** **Read the following questions, then listen to the text once more and answer them.**

1. What happened in 1830?

   ..............................................................................................................

2. What happened to many of the 100,000 Native Americans on their way to Oklahoma?

   ..............................................................................................................

3. In what respect were the Native Americans' children separated from their traditional life?

   ..............................................................................................................

4. What was the big problem in the year 1890?

   ..............................................................................................................

5. What did the soldiers originally want to do in South Dakota in 1890?

   ..............................................................................................................

6. How many people lost their lives in the Wounded Knee Massacre?

   ..............................................................................................................

7. Why can the Wounded Knee Massacre be seen as a turning point in the history of intercultural relations in North America?

   ..............................................................................................................

**Exercise 3** **Complete the following sentences. If necessary, listen to the text once more.**

1. American Indians had lived in North America long before ......................................
2. In 1876 the rest of the American Indians had to move to reservations because ..........

   ..............................................................................................................

3. The Native Americans began to protest because ..........................................

   ..............................................................................................................

4. The peaceful "Ghost Dance" sometimes lasted ..........................................
5. The American people were shocked when ..........................................

   ..............................................................................................................

6. After the massacre the American Indians gave ..........................................

   ..............................................................................................................

**Anmerkung:** Auf der nächsten Seite findest du den gedruckten Text „Wounded Knee". Blättere jedoch nicht um, bevor du die Aufgaben 1–3 zum Hörverstehen gemacht hast!

*Lösungen Seite 121*

**Tipp zum Leseverstehen:** Halte beim Erarbeiten eines Lesetexts stets verschiedenfarbige Stifte bereit. Markiere dir beim Lesen unbekannte Wörter, die du nicht erschließen kannst, die du aber zum Verständnis brauchst und daher in einem Wörterbuch nachschlagen musst. Außerdem solltest du dir wesentliche Inhalte, wichtige Textstellen und Schlüsselwörter markieren; das erleichtert dir später die Beantwortung der Fragen.

**Exercise 4** **Read the following text and answer the questions on the next page using your own words.**

## Wounded Knee

Native Americans had lived in the United States long before the 'white man' arrived from Europe. But as more and more settlers came, the US government needed more land in the east. So in 1830, President Andrew Jackson passed a law – the Indian Removal Act. This law allowed the government to buy land from Native Americans. The Native Americans were 'removed' and given land further west, in the Oklahoma area. The law said that the Native Americans didn't have to sell their land. But in reality, the government forced them – soldiers were sent to organize the removal of about 100,000 Native Americans, many of whom became sick or died on the long march west.

Soon the US needed even more land – and in 1876, the rest of the Native Americans were forced to move to special 'reservations'. Here they were separated from their traditional life and forced to live like European Americans; for example, they had to send their children to boarding schools. At school the children were not allowed to learn about Native American culture or speak their native languages. Another problem was food: the Native Americans couldn't hunt in the reservations, and they were forced to farm like Europeans. These problems came to a climax in the year 1890 when the weather was very hot and there wasn't enough rain to grow food. Life became impossibly hard for the Native Americans and they began to protest.

Part of the protest was a dance called the 'Ghost Dance'. The dance came from an Indian spiritual leader called Wovoka, who believed that Native Americans could live beside the 'white man' in peace. Many Native Americans took part in the peaceful dance – a dance which sometimes lasted for three or four days. But the European settlers didn't understand it – they thought that it was a war dance and that the Native Americans wanted to attack them. So in December, 1890, the government sent soldiers to South Dakota, where many spiritual leaders lived, to stop the dancing.

The soldiers' plan was to move the Native Americans from South Dakota further south to Nebraska. On December 29$^{th}$, a group of Sioux Indians were taken by five hundred US soldiers to Wounded Knee, South Dakota. The soldiers wanted the Sioux to give them their guns, but there were arguments. The soldiers and the Indians were nervous, and suddenly a battle started. The battle lasted only five minutes, but when the shooting had stopped, about three hundred Sioux Indian men, women and children had been massacred by US soldiers. In comparison, only about twenty-five US soldiers died in the battle.

People all over the country soon heard the news of the massacre – the nation was shocked at what the military had done. After the massacre, Native American leaders stopped protesting. They gave their guns to the military and the Wounded Knee Massacre was the last armed conflict between Native Americans and US soldiers.

 *Lösungen Seite 122*

***Info:*** *Today 2.1 million Native Americans live in the US, mostly in Alaska, New Mexico, South Dakota, Oklahoma, Montana, North Dakota and Arizona. The names of some states come from 'Indian' words. For example, Oklahoma comes from the Choctaw Indians and means 'red people'. And Kentucky is an Iroquois word that means 'land of tomorrow'. Michigan, the name of another state, is also an Indian word, which means 'great or large lake' – and Lake Michigan is one of the five Great Lakes (Lake Michigan, Lake Erie, Lake Huron, Lake Superior and Lake Ontario).*

**Questions on the text:**

1. What rights were written down in the Indian Removal Act?
2. Why did the Indians take part in the "Ghost Dance"?
3. How did the Wounded Knee Massacre come about?
4. In what respect have the Native Americans left their mark on the map of the USA?

**Exercise 5** **Now match the following synonyms with expressions from the text.**

give someone the right to do something – ..........

take/send someone away from a place – ..........

make someone do something – ..........

without war and fighting – ..........

conflicts/fights with words – ..........

killing in which many people die on one side – ..........

the people of a country – ..........

using weapons – ..........

*Lösungen Seite 122*

## 7.2 National Parks

Jenny has also found an interesting text about national parks.

**Exercise 1** **Go to www.gute-noten-in.de/lernen/en/8/audio and listen to the audio "National Parks". *Shut this book* and do not open it as long as you are listening for the first time!**
**Just try to understand the main ideas of the text to able to complete the sentence.**

The text is about ..................................................................................................................

.................................................................................................................................................

.................................................................................................................................................

**Exercise 2** **Listen to the text again and fill in the gaps.**

### National Parks

In the 19th century, industry was expanding in the US. America wanted to protect its .........................................................., and in 1864, it became the first country in the world to officially do this. President Abraham Lincoln signed an important law that said ............................................... should only be used for recreation and that they should be open for everyone to use. This law created something the world had never seen before – ...................................................... .

The very first one was Yellowstone National Park. It was created on March 1st, 1872, and is located in the western states of Wyoming, Montana and Idaho. The park is home



*Lösungen Seite 122/123*

to .......................................... like grizzly bears, wolves and bison. And there are about 600 species of .............................. and .............................. there! Around 2.8 million visitors come to Yellowstone every year to see the world's most famous geyser, 'Old Faithful'. Every 90 minutes, the geyser shoots up to 32,000 liters of hot water into the air.

Yellowstone is big – it has an area of 8,983 km². Back in 1872, there were no formal park regulations for visitors. Also, there weren't enough .........................................., and the first park manager worked for five years for free because there wasn't enough money to pay him. The lack of ...................................... made it very difficult to ........................................ the park, and very often people stole natural resources and hunted animals .......................................... . Soon the .................................................... realized that it had to do something. It provided money for the world's first park ranger, Harry Yount. But Harry left a year later – he said the job was too difficult for one man. Almost ten years later, in 1886, they called in the army to help look after the park.

The army managed the park for an amazing thirty-two years! It developed regulations for the .......................................... of the park. And thanks to the army, many species of wildlife were saved from .............................................. . In 1916, the army's job was finished, and they gave control of the park to a new organization – the ............................................................ .................................. (NPS). Today park rangers are an important part of the NPS: they report ............................................ and stop people from ........................................... the park. They can also carry guns, like the police. Park rangers have their own uniforms, and they wear hats called 'Ranger Stetsons', which are much like the old army hats.

Including Yellowstone, there are 58 national parks in the US today. Famous national parks include Badlands National Park in South Dakota, Yosemite National Park in California, Grand Canyon National Park in Arizona, and Rocky Mountain National Park in Colorado. And .......................................... states like Alaska and Hawaii also have their own national parks. Some people say that national parks were the ......................................... America ever had. And other countries thought so, too, so today there are national parks all over the world.

**Annotations:** ***to expand*** (sich) ausdehnen · ***recreation*** Erholung · ***faithful*** treu, verlässlich · ***regulation*** Regel · ***lack*** Mangel · ***park ranger*** Parkaufseher · ***Stetson***® berühmter Hersteller US-amerikanischer (Cowboy-)Hüte

*Lösungen Seite 123*

**Exercise 3** **Read the text carefully – after having corrected possible mistakes – and answer the following questions in keywords, using your own words.**

1. Why had it become necessary in the 19th century to protect nature?

.................................................................................................................................

2. What was the law Abraham Lincoln signed in 1864 about?

.................................................................................................................................

.................................................................................................................................

3. What is Yellowstone National Park famous for?

.................................................................................................................................

.................................................................................................................................

4. What problems had to be solved during the first years of Yellowstone's existence?

.................................................................................................................................

.................................................................................................................................

5. What was the army needed for, and what did they achieve by 1916?

.................................................................................................................................

.................................................................................................................................

6. Why are park rangers, according to the text, so important for the national parks?

.................................................................................................................................

.................................................................................................................................

7. In how far was the idea of national parks not only a national achievement?

.................................................................................................................................

.................................................................................................................................



*Lösungen Seite 123*

## 7.3 American English versus British English

As you may have recognised, the two texts of this chapter are – unlike all the others – written in American English. Between British and American English, there are differences in pronunciation, spelling, vocabulary and grammar. As far as pronunciation is concerned, you will notice the differences if you listen carefully to the previous two listening texts (www.gute-noten-in.de/lernen/en/8/audio).

**Alles klar?!** ***Differences in Spelling***

Zu den wichtigsten Unterschieden in den Schreibung von amerikanischem und britischem Englisch zählen:

| British English | American English |
|---|---|
| ***-re:*** | ***-er:*** |
| *centre, litre, metre, theatre* | *center, liter, meter, theater* |
| ***-our:*** | ***-or:*** |
| *behaviour, colour, flavour, humour* | *behavior, color, flavor, humor* |
| ***-ce:*** | ***-se*** |
| *defence, licence (= noun!), offence* | *defense, license, offense* |
| ***-ogue:*** | ***-og:*** |
| *catalogue, dialogue* | *catalog, dialog* |
| ***-ise, -isation:*** | ***-ize, -ization:*** |
| *realise, recognise, globalisation* | *realize, recognize, globalization* |

**Alles klar?!** ***Differences in Vocabulary***

Es ist wichtig zu wissen, dass es im *British English* und *American English* für viele Dinge verschiedene Wörter gibt. Diese Unterschiede im Wortschatz solltest du dir einprägen. Häufig verwendete Wörter sind:

| | ***British English*** | ***American English*** |
|---|---|---|
| Herbst | *autumn* | *fall* |
| Keks | *biscuit* | *cookie* |
| Pommes frites | *chips* | *(French) fries* |
| Kino | *cinema* | *movie theater* |
| Chips | *crisps* | *chips* |
| Führerschein | *driving licence* | *driver's license* |
| (Schul-/Übungs-)Heft | *exercise book* | *notebook* |
| Film | *film* | *movie* |
| Wohnung | *flat* | *apartment* |
| Fußball(spiel/match) | *football (match)* | *soccer (game)* |
| Garten | *garden* | *yard* |
| Erdgeschoss | *ground floor* | *first floor* |
| Urlaub | *holiday* | *vacation* |
| Aufzug | *lift* | *elevator* |
| Lastwagen | *lorry* | *truck* |
| Note | *mark* | *grade* |
| Autobahn | *motorway* | *freeway* |
| gemein | *nasty* | *mean* |
| Bürgersteig | *pavement* | *sidewalk* |
| Benzin | *petrol* | *gas* |
| Post(bote) | *post(man)* | *mail(man)* |
| Privatschule | *public school* | *private school* |
| Schüler | *pupil* | *student* |
| (Warte-)Schlange | *queue* | *line* |
| Eisenbahn | *railway* | *railroad* |
| Radiergummi | *rubber* | *eraser* |
| Müll | *rubbish* | *garbage* |
| Rucksack | *rucksack* | *backpack* |
| Geschäft | *shop* | *store* |
| staatliche Schule | *state school* | *public school* |
| Süßigkeiten | *sweets* | *candy* |
| Stundenplan, Fahrplan | *timetable* | *schedule* |
| Dose | *tin* | *can* |
| Toilette | *toilet* | *restroom* |
| Hose | *trousers* | *pants* |
| U-Bahn | *underground* | *subway* |
| Unterhose | *(under)pants* | *shorts* |
| 5. Klasse (= Jahrgangsstufe!) | *year 5* | *$5^{th}$ grade* |

**Exercise 1** **Complete the crossword puzzle with the American English equivalent of the British English word given.**

American English word for BE *rubbish bin*:

flat
lorry
rubber
petrol
crisps
sweets
autumn
queue

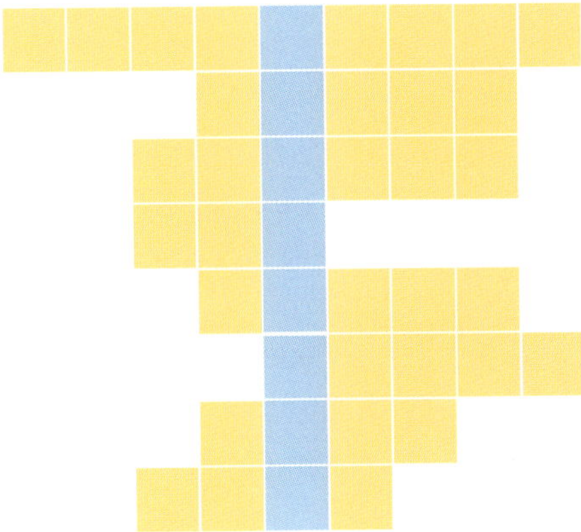

**Exercise 2** ★ **Rewrite the following sentences changing the American English words into British English.**

1. San Francisco is my favorite city in the States. I would like to have an apartment there.

2. Yesterday I went to the movie theater instead of watching a soccer game on TV.

3. We are planning a barbecue in our back yard for next week. Would you like fries with your steak?

4. Have you seen the new candy store? They have lots of different cookies.

5. When I was in 7th grade, I always had good grades.

*Lösungen Seite 124*

**Alles klar?!** ***Differences in Grammar***

Die grammatikalischen Unterschiede sind vergleichsweise gering bzw. nicht immer eindeutig zuzuordnen.

Zu den auffälligsten Unterschieden gehören:

- die unterschiedliche Verwendung von *present perfect* und *simple past*: Im ***American English*** wird **mit** den Adverbien ***yet, already*** und ***just*** nicht das *present perfect*, sondern das ***simple past*** verwendet.
- die Verwendung unregelmäßiger Verben: Manche Verben besitzen sowohl regelmäßige als auch unregelmäßige Formen. Während im ***British English*** eher die **unregelmäßigen Formen** verwendet werden, bevorzugt man im ***American English*** tendenziell die **regelmäßigen Formen**.

**Exercise 3** **Look at the following sentences and decide whether they are British or American English.**

| | BE | AE |
|---|---|---|
| That street was really dirty, with garbage everywhere. | | |
| Tom was standing in a queue waiting to get into the lift. | | |
| What is your favourite song? | | |
| I couldn't go to the theatre yesterday. | | |
| They know all about it because I already spoke to them. | | |
| You must not park on the pavement. | | |
| Last night I dreamed of a new car. | | |
| The mailbox is over there on the right, in front of the drugstore. | | |
| Mr Black lives on the first floor, so he needn't climb up any stairs. | | |
| Did you see the new catalog yet? | | |



*Lösungen Seite 124*

# Test your Progress (20 minutes)

**Exercise 1** **Complete the crossword puzzle with the British English equivalent of the American English word.**

British English word for AE *downtown*:

movie theater
railroad
mail
mean
backpack
pants
yard
schedule
freeway
sidewalk

Points: ☐ out of 10

**Exercise 2** **Change the following British English sentences into American English.**

1. You can take the underground [to the] city centre. *(Klammer nicht übersetzen!)*

   ..........................................................................................

2. I have already spelt my name twice.

   ..........................................................................................

3. Do you like the new flavour?

   ..........................................................................................

4. When I was young, his flat was above the shop.

   ..........................................................................................

5. Our new car needs less petrol.

   ..........................................................................................

6. In the $21^{st}$ century you cannot stop globalisation any more.

   ..........................................................................................

Points: ☐ out of 9

*Lösungen Seite 125*

**Exercise 3** **Jenny's e-mail friend Linda from New York has sent her a holiday postcard. Change her American English into British English.**

Dear Jenny,

Up to now our vacation here in California was fantastic. Yesterday we visited Yosemite National Park. It is open all year round, but in fall, when the colors of the leaves are incredibly impressive, most of the visitors come here for hiking. The most spectacular rock here is called 'Half Dome' and it is more than 2,500 meters high. Perhaps you already saw it in a movie?

In the park you have to be very careful about black bears. You must not throw away any garbage because they smell and look for everything from leftover cookies to empty beer cans. But with the right behavior you can enjoy the beauty of nature in Yosemite Park.

You must come here and see it all by yourself!

Yours, Linda

Points: ☐ out of 11

Total points: ☐ out of 30

27–30: Super! Du beherrschst die Unterschiede zwischen *British English* und *American English* schon sehr gut!

15–26: Teilweise kannst du mit den Unterschieden von *British English* und *American English* schon recht gut umgehen, aber oft machst du noch Fehler. Wiederhole diesen Abschnitt noch einmal!

0–14: Die richtige Unterscheidung zwischen *British English* und *American English* bereitet dir noch große Probleme. Wiederhole diesen Abschnitt gründlich und mache die Übungen konzentriert noch einmal.


*Lösungen Seite 125*

# 8 Games and Puzzles

Next Saturday is Jenny and Peter's birthday, and they are planning their birthday party. This year they want to invite their friends for a "Gaming Night". And apart from snacks and drinks, they are preparing lots of funny games and puzzles.

Join them and enjoy yourselves!

## 8.1 Dominoes – Gerund or Infinitive?

**Alles klar?!** ***How to Play the Game***

**Preparation:** Copy the domino cards on this and the following page and cut them up. You can play this game with your friends in a group of 3 to 5 pupils. Each player gets 5 cards. The rest of the cards are put face down on the table in a pile, the "stock pile".

**Start playing:** The youngest player starts by putting one "domino" card on the table. The next player arranges his/her card next to it forming a grammatically correct sentence. The other players decide whether it is grammatically correct (if you are not sure, you can look it up in chapter 3). If it is, the next player can take his/her turn. If it is wrong, the pupil has to take his/her card back, plus an additional one from the pile. If he/she still has no suitable card to add, he/she also has to take a second additional card from the pile.

**End of the game:** The first player to get rid of all his/her "dominoes" is the winner. Have fun!

| | | | | |
|---|---|---|---|---|
| … to hurt you. | … working hard and neatly. | … to solve the puzzle in vain. | … going by train. | … to have a good job in five years' time. |
| Mr and Mrs Wilson love … | Peter hates … | Her friends enjoy … | Peter's hobby is … | Thomas is very interested in … |
| … drinking coffee. | … going to the dentist. | … singing | … playing the guitar. | … reading books about other countries. |
| I don't mind … | Mr Wilson is really good at … | Anne hates … | Don't risk … | I don't feel like … |
| … jogging at 6 am. | … skiing. | … eating pizza. | … losing your job. | … walking in the rain. |
| I'm looking forward to … | Jenny is crazy about … | Peter really loves … | Thomas never succeeds in … | Anne is very keen on … |

| | | | | |
|---|---|---|---|---|
| … meeting you again. | … reading books. | … playing with Rex. | … getting to school on time. | … dancing. |
| Mr Wilson wants … | Mrs Wilson loves … | Jenny, you are really bad at … | Tim promised … | Boris never succeeds in … |
| … to give up smoking. | … sunbathing. | … lying. | … to call me tomorrow evening. | … getting a good mark in maths. |
| Richard asked me … | Jenny is sick of … | Thomas would like … | Mrs Wilson wants her children … | Jenny and Peter want … |
| … to come to his party. | … getting up early. | … to spend a year abroad. | … to do their homework properly. | … to get more pocket money. |
| There is no reason for … | You have to take the opportunity of … | It's no good … | I expect you … | Peter has decided … |
| … getting angry. | … learning a foreign language. | … wasting your money on expensive shoes. | … to win that match. | … to join the drama group. |
| Mrs Wilson doesn't allow Jenny … | All their friends are invited … | I have warned you … | Thomas has worked very hard … | Mr Wilson is thinking about when … |
| … to go out late at night. | … to come to their birthday party. | … not to come home late. | … to pass his exam. | … to make an appointment at the dentist. |
| Peter was the first one … | I'd prefer … | Don't forget … | I can't remember … | After breakfast I went on … |
| … to finish his project. | … drinking a cup of coffee. | … to close the windows before you leave. | … seeing that film. | … to work in the garden. |
| I never meant … | Being a good pupil means … | I have tried … | If there is a traffic jam, you could try … | Thomas hopes … |

## 8.2 Crossword Puzzle

phrasal verb for *to chase (so.)*:

to be as proud as a ...

phrasal verb for *to reject*

English word for *engagiert*

synonym for *to give in*

... wine (with bubbles of gas)

"... your shoes before you come in!"

AE word for *toilet*

famous national park in the USA

phrasal verb for *to tidy*

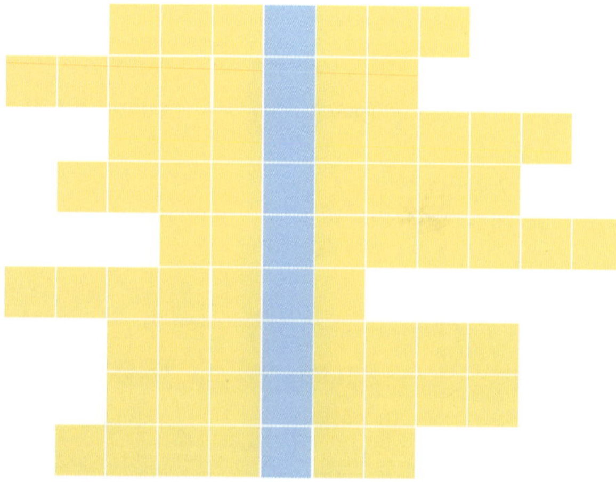

## 8.3 Taboo

**Alles klar?!** ***How to Play the Game***

**Preparation:** Copy the cards on the following page and cut them up. The cards are put face down on the table in a pile. You need at least 4 players, divided in 2 groups of at least 2 people each (but the more you are, the better!). Taboo is played in rounds of 1 minute, which the teams take in turns. During a round, one group explains/guesses the "taboo" words, and the other group checks whether the rules are observed by the opponent. In the next round, the other group becomes the explaining/guessing group.

**Start playing:** The oldest player takes a card and tries to explain the expression on the top to his group members without using any of the expressions below it; the group members keep shouting out their guesses. If the person explaining the word uses one of the "taboo" words on the card by mistake, the opponent group gets the point. If the explaining player's group can guess the word, they get the point; if not, the other group gets the point. When the minute is up, it is the other group's turn to do the explaining. Play the game, with a member of the opposing team timing one minute and shouting *"Stop!"* when the minute is up.

**End of the game:** When all the cards have been played, when a certain number of rounds has been played or when a certain number of points has been reached, the group with the most points is the winner.
Have fun!



*Lösungen Seite 126*

| | | | | |
|---|---|---|---|---|
| **mashed potatoes** | **sparkling water** | **fruit salad** | **championship** | **dancing** |
| to eat<br>chips<br>to boil<br>fish | bubbles<br>tap<br>bottle<br>gas | apple<br>banana<br>strawberry<br>to mix | football<br>world<br>score<br>goal | music<br>step<br>disco<br>ballet |
| **computer** | **e-mail** | **butterfly** | **bee** | **map** |
| screen<br>laptop<br>programme<br>crash | send<br>receive<br>computer<br>reply | summer<br>colour<br>caterpillar<br>beautiful | honey<br>busy<br>flower<br>sting | earth<br>city<br>way<br>orientation |
| **mobile phone** | **Native Americans** | **Wounded Knee** | **national park** | **park ranger** |
| call<br>text message<br>number<br>battery | USA<br>Winnetou<br>reservation<br>Red Indian | Indians<br>massacre<br>soldiers<br>to die | nature<br>to protect<br>wildlife<br>animals | national park<br>uniform<br>rules<br>to control |
| **Yellowstone** | **tree** | **flat** | **garden** | **teacher** |
| national park<br>bears<br>geyser<br>nature | plant<br>trunk<br>leaves<br>big | house<br>room<br>to live<br>rent | to play<br>plants<br>lawn<br>back | school<br>class<br>pupil<br>to mark |
| **underground** | **hobby** | **party** | **author** | **kingdom** |
| city<br>to go<br>transport<br>ticket | playing<br>dancing<br>singing<br>cooking | to dance<br>music<br>birthday<br>fun | to write<br>book<br>novel<br>literature | queen<br>Great Britain<br>monarchy<br>England |

## 8.4 The Wilson Family's Board Game

**Alles klar?!** ***How to Play the Game***

**Preparation:** Copy (and if possible, enlarge) the following game board. You need a dice and one counter for each player.

**Start playing:** The players throw the dice and move their counters according to the number. If the player whose turn it is can solve the task, he/she may stay on the square; if not, he/she has to move back to the previous square.

The first player to reach FINISH is the winner.
Good Luck!

| | | | | |
|---|---|---|---|---|
| **START** | 1<br>**Will or going-to future?**<br>I ... (do) my homework tomorrow. | 2<br>**Article or no article?**<br>I didn't know that Tim was such ... fool. | 3<br>**You are lucky!**<br>It is your birthday today. Move 2 squares. | 4<br>**Gerund or infinitive?**<br>Mr Wilson enjoys ... (tell) jokes. |
| 9<br>**Correct the mistake.**<br>Thomas has been never to the USA. | 8<br>**Have a break.**<br>Skip a turn. | 7<br>**Complete with a preposition.**<br>I'm afraid the batteries are running .... | 6<br>**Since or for?**<br>Richard hasn't been at the youth club ... last weekend. | 5<br>**Change into American English.**<br>She loves biscuits. |
| 10<br>**Fill in the correct tense.**<br>We won't go on holiday if you ... (be) ill. | 11<br>**Make or do?**<br>Who wants to ... the shopping today? | 12<br>**Bad luck!**<br>You have lost your keys. Move back 2 squares. | 13<br>**Correct the word order.**<br>We/at 8 o'clock/ at the club/met. | 14<br>**Fill in the correct form.**<br>Listen! The police ... (come). |
| 19<br>**You are lucky!**<br>You have passed your exam. Move 2 squares. | 18<br>**Infinitive or participle?**<br>The man ... (stand) there is my uncle. | 17<br>**Article or no article?**<br>Today children learn to respect ... nature. | 16<br>**Present perfect or simple past?**<br>Jenny ... (not – call) Anne yet. | 15<br>**Complete the idiom.**<br>This trip has been the best thing since .... |
| 20<br>**Bad luck!**<br>You forgot to lay the table. Move back 2 squares. | 21<br>**Singular or plural?**<br>The USA is/are really great! | 22<br>**Correct the mistake.**<br>I think I'll become a bike for my birthday. | 23<br>**Fill in the correct tense.**<br>If you ... (work) hard, you would pass the text. | **FINISH** |



*Lösungen Seite 126*

# Lösungen

## 1.1 Revision of Present and Past Tenses

**Exercise 1** (Seite 8)

1. When Mrs Wilson came home from her job interview, Mr Wilson was preparing dinner.
2. Mr Wilson was peeling potatoes when his mobile phone rang.
3. At 2 o'clock Jenny was writing a text message to Anne on her new mobile phone.
4. Thomas had to lie down because he had a bad headache.
5. Rex was nervous when the ambulance drove past.

**Exercise 2** (Seite 8)

1. Jenny and Peter are both in year 8 now. They have chosen German as a foreign language.
2. Jenny's best friend Anne is also in their class.
3. Thomas is in the sixth form; he is studying for his A-levels.
4. Thomas has never been to Canada, but he wants to go there after finishing school.
5. What was he doing last night at ten o'clock? – He was playing the guitar.
6. Mrs Wilson has been looking for an interesting job since she lost her job as a translator last year.
7. Apart from being a housewife at the moment, she started a course for web page design six months ago.
8. Mr Wilson likes cooking and has promised to prepare a roast turkey for tonight.

## 1.2 Revision of Future Tenses

**Exercise** (Seite 10)

Jenny, Peter and their friends are talking about their holiday plans.

Jenny: I think I will get a holiday job at a café. I am going to ask at several cafés in the neighbourhood. I am taking/going to take part in a dancing workshop in summer; my parents have lent me the money for it. It starts in June, and perhaps I will win the competition in August.

Peter: I will probably do an extra maths course. I know that it won't be much fun, but it's necessary. Apart from that I am going to play football whenever possible. On Friday 5th, Chelsea will be playing, and I've got tickets! So from about 8 pm I will be sitting in the stadium.

Anne: I am going to join my cousin Jill on her trip to Spain; my parents have allowed it! My mother is going to have/is having a baby, so she won't travel a lot this year. But by next year, we will all have got used to the baby, so maybe we will fly to Greece then.

Tim: I am going to take part in a circus project. It takes place in the first holiday week, from 9 am to 4 pm every day. We will be training all week long, and the performance starts at 3 pm on Saturday. My parents and friends are going to come/are coming to watch it. Do you also want to see it?

## Test your Progress

**Exercise 1** (Seite 11)

1. Uncle Harry has always lived in Liverpool.
2. Mrs Wilson has bought a new hat. Isn't it beautiful?
3. On June 5th in the morning, Thomas will be taking his A-levels in maths.

4. Did you play football when you were a boy?
5. Peter was lying in hospital when his father bought the new car last Saturday.
6. The plane has just taken off; it will be in New York in 7 hours.
7. While Mrs Wilson was making the cake yesterday, Jenny was doing her homework.
8. I am going to read this book soon.

**Exercise 2** (Seite 11)

Last weekend Peter visited his Uncle Harry in Liverpool. Now he is telling Jenny about it. "I had told Uncle Harry that I would arrive at 11 am, but then my train was late. Fortunately, he was waiting at the station when I finally arrived. We walked to the Cathedral, where I climbed to the top. Uncle Harry had been there so many times that he did not come with me; he had a coffee at the Cathedral coffee shop instead. I had heard a lot about the Beatles' first concerts, so we also went to see the famous Cavern Club, where a band was practising for a concert. I hope we will go there again on my next visit."

**Exercise 3** (Seite 12)

Jenny, Peter and Thomas are planning their weekend.

Thomas: Have you decided yet what you want to do on Saturday, Peter?
Peter: Well, I talked to Aunt Helen on the phone yesterday, and she said she would like to come over.
Jenny: Probably the weather will be nice. So we could take her on a walk to the National Gallery and show her the painting exhibition.
Peter: I think there won't be enough time, as her train arrives at half past four and the exhibition ends at five o'clock.
Jenny: That's a pity. How about a party for Aunt Helen? We have not seen her for months, and it will be her birthday anyway.
Peter: How old will she be?
Jenny: 45, I think.
Thomas: Well, perhaps I will paint a picture of her as a surprise present.
Peter: But be careful, she will be rather angry if the picture isn't good.
Jenny: How about visiting Greenwich and the Royal Observatory on Sunday? I am reading a book about its history at the moment, and it sounds really interesting.
Peter: Have you ever been there, Thomas?
Thomas: Oh, yes, I was there when I was little, but I can hardly remember. So why not go there?
Jenny: That sounds good. I think it will be an interesting weekend!

## 2.1 Conditional Sentences – Types I, II and III

**Exercise 1** (Seite 14)

1. If you come to the club, we will/can meet.
2. If Anne goes there, too, Jenny will/can show Richard to her.
3. It might rain if they leave very late.
4. If it rains too much, Richard won't/might not/may not come.
5. Will I recognize him if I don't wear my glasses?
6. If you finish your homework soon, help me in the kitchen, please.
7. Anne will help Jenny with German if she needs her.
8. If Thomas passes his maths test, he may/will go on a weekend trip with his friends.

## Exercise 2 (Seite 15)

1. If you knew Richard, you would agree that he is really handsome.
2. You would catch the bus if you left in time.
3. If Thomas took driving lessons, he could drive a car.
4. If Jenny thought reasonably, she would eat something.
5. It would be better if you waited for me.
6. Jenny would come if Richard invited her.
7. If the youth club was closed, what would we do?
8. If Mr Wilson played the lottery, he might win a million.

## Exercise 3 (Seite 16)

1. If Richard hadn't forgotten Jenny's birthday, he would have invited her to the cinema.
2. If Peter had learnt enough English, he wouldn't have failed the test.
3. If Thomas had been at home before midnight, his parents wouldn't have been angry.
4. Anne wouldn't have broken into the frozen river if she had been careful.
5. If you had asked me, I could have helped you.
6. If Thomas had seen the bus, he wouldn't have been injured in an accident.

## Exercise 4 (Seite 17)

(1.–2. If Anne had caught the bus to the youth club, Jenny would have met her there.)
2.–3. If Jenny had met her there, they would have gone to the cinema together.
3.–4. If they had gone to the cinema together, Thomas would have been waiting for them there.
4.–5. If Thomas had been waiting for them there, he would have asked Anne to go out with him.
5.–6. If he had asked Anne to go out with him, they would have spent a wonderful evening together.
6.–7. If they had spent a wonderful evening together, she would have come home after midnight.
7.–8. If she had come home after midnight, she would have overslept the next day.

## Exercise 5 (Seite 17)

1. If Peter's friend Daniel from Munich comes for a visit next summer, the Wilsons will show him all the famous sights in London.
2. If Daniel's parents came, too, Mr and Mrs Wilson would take them to one of the many theatres in the West End to see a musical.
3. "We will/can walk through Hyde Park if the weather is fine;
   if you ever get lost, just look at this map."
4. If Daniel is (was) interested in arts, they can/will visit (could/would visit) the Tate Modern, a great gallery of modern art.
5. They could make a trip to Brighton on the south coast if Daniel stayed for more than a week.
6. "If I were/(was) you, I would stay here for at least one month."
7. If Daniel had known that staying with the Wilsons was so much fun, he would have visited them earlier.

## 2.2 Conditional Sentences – Mixed Types

**Exercise** (Seite 18)

1. Peter wouldn't be such a good football player if he had not started playing/to play at the age of four.
2. If Jenny wasn't a talented dancer, she couldn't have taken part in the workshop.
3. If Anne left home only three minutes ago, she will be late for school.
4. If Mr Wilson had not had an accident, he wouldn't have a broken leg now.
5. I'm sure Richard would have invited Jenny if he knew her better.
6. If Peter was more reliable, he could have borrowed his brother's bike.
7. If Mr Wilson had bought the ring, he would have a birthday present for his wife now.
8. If the shop closed at 6 o'clock, we won't get any salt-and-vinegar crisps for the party tonight.

## Test your Progress

**Exercise 1** (Seite 19)

| | | |
|---|---|---|
| If I lend you the money, | you will spend it on clothes.<br>you spent it on clothes.<br>you would have spent it on clothes. | ✔<br><br> |
| You would not be at the party | if I did not invite you.<br>if I had not invited you.<br>if I would not have invited you. | <br>✔<br> |
| If you want to be successful, | you might work hard.<br>you will have to work hard.<br>you would have to work hard. | <br>✔<br> |
| If Peter wanted to go to the football match, | his father would take him there.<br>his father took him there.<br>his father will take him there. | ✔<br><br> |
| Jenny only asks her mother for advice | if she was not sure herself.<br>if she is not sure herself.<br>if she had not been sure herself. | <br>✔<br> |
| Would Jenny and Anne have become friends | if they lived in the same house?<br>if they live in the same house?<br>if they had lived in the same house? | ✔<br><br>✔ |
| If you try hard, | you may become a famous dancer.<br>you will become a famous dancer.<br>you would become a famous dancer. | ✔<br>✔<br> |

### Exercise 2 (Seite 19/20)

1. Jenny and Anne, if you walk all the way home in the middle of the night, something terrible might happen.
2. Peter, if you stay at the disco after midnight, the police will take you home.
3. What would you do if a stranger asked you where you were going?
4. If my mother asked me to do all the housework, I would move out!
5. If a stranger had offered me some chocolate when I was a child, I certainly wouldn't have taken it.
6. I would run away if my parents told me to marry a rich man.
7. If Mr and Mrs Wilson hadn't met at a party 20 years ago, Thomas, Jenny and Peter wouldn't have been born.
8. If you join the youth club, you can come to the disco every week.

### Exercise 3 (Seite 20)

1. Anne would buy those jeans if they were not so expensive.
2. If the weather is fine, I will play tennis.
3. If you had read the instructions before, you would know how to use the camera.
4. If the pupils are attentive, there won't be any homework.
5. If he doesn't shut the window, we will die of cold.
6. Peter would have been killed if the bus hadn't stopped.
7. If Mrs Wilson didn't know how to work with the computer, she wouldn't have had so many job interviews yet.
8. If you want to have dinner soon, lay the table, please.
9. Mum would be very angry with us if we took her mobile phone without asking.
10. Call before ten o'clock if you want me to drive you home.
11. If the telephone hadn't rung, the cake wouldn't have been burnt.
12. If I succeed in the exam, I will be very proud!

## 3.1 The Gerund

### Exercise 1 (Seite 22)

*Lösungsvorschlag:*

1. Swimming is healthy.
2. Playing football is exhausting.
3. Singing is fun.
4. Travelling is expensive.
5. Skiing is dangerous.
6. Painting is boring.
7. Riding a horse (oder: horse-riding) is difficult.
8. Reading is interesting.

### Exercise 2 (Seite 23)

1. Jenny sometimes enjoys playing football with her brother Peter.
2. Why does Anne avoid meeting her German teacher?
3. Last week her German teacher considered giving Anne a bad mark.
4. Give up smoking, Dad!
5. Mrs Wilson: "Does the job involve translating interesting texts?"
6. Thomas will finish practising for the concert soon.
7. "Thomas, have you ever suggested travelling to Canada with your new girlfriend?"
8. Anne: "I could not imagine being an actress."

**Exercise 3** (Seite 26)

1. Jenny is excited about performing a modern dance tonight.
2. After having dinner, the Wilson family will go and see Jenny dance.
3. "There is no reason for being (so) nervous."
4. "I'm not used to taking part in a dancing competition."
5. Richard is glad about coming (oder: having come) to see her performance.
6. Jenny is very proud of winning (oder: having won) the competition.

**Exercise 4** (Seite 26)

1. Anne insists on going to the club to tell everybody of Jenny's triumph.
2. Jenny is usually keen on dancing in the disco. Today she even feels like singing for her friends.
3. Will I have the opportunity of talking to Richard at the club?
4. Thomas is looking forward to playing at the concert next week; he is tired of practising every day.
5. Peter is not used to playing as a goalkeeper. He is afraid of losing the next match.
6. The Wilsons are planning their holiday. They are thinking of travelling to the USA. They have the choice between driving along the west coast on Highway 1 or experiencing the Indian Summer in New England in the east. Jenny is interested in seeing American skyscrapers.
7. Anne will be responsible for feeding the cat when the Wilsons are on holiday. She will also have to think of watering the plants.

**Exercise 5** (Seite 27)

1. Jenny and Anne are keen on going to Thomas's concert.
2. "Look over there! I'm happy about seeing that Richard is here, too!"
3. "Hi Jenny, congratulations! You are famous for dancing now.
4. "Thank you! But I am bad at playing the guitar, whereas Thomas is so good at playing it.
5. Richard doesn't know a reason for not asking Jenny to go to the cinema with him.
6. Do you feel like watching the romantic comedy they are showing at the Odeon?
7. "Yes, I am looking forward to watching the film next week!"

**Exercise 6** (Seite 27)

1. After winning the match, Peter's coach thanked him for defending the goal so well.
2. "Mother has just succeeded in getting a well-paid new job!"
3. Peter is disappointed about not getting the main part in the school play.
4. Mr Wilson accused Peter of using his laptop to go online without asking.
5. Mrs Wilson does not agree with postponing the meeting.

**Exercise 7** (Seite 28)

1. It was worth going to Thomas's concert.
2. Jenny can't help thinking of Richard all the time.
3. It's no use denying that the boy who plays the main part is/was very good at acting.
4. Thomas can't help feeling anxious about the grammar test tomorrow.
5. It's no good complaining about not getting enough pocket money.
6. How about going out for dinner tonight?

## 3.2 The to-Infinitive

**Exercise 1** (Seite 30)

1. Jenny hopes to know Richard's telephone number by tomorrow.
2. Mr Wilson expects Thomas to pass his A-level exams.
3. Yesterday Mrs Wilson told Jenny not to get her new jacket dirty.
4. Last Saturday Peter promised to be home before 11 pm.
5. The doctor wants Mr Wilson to give up smoking.
6. Mother will never allow Jenny to go to the disco next weekend.
7. We have decided to go on holiday to Maine and watch whales next summer.
8. Jenny, would you like to join the choir?

**Exercise 2** (Seite 30)

Jenny tells Thomas about the drama group: "At the beginning our teacher tells us to listen to his instructions. He wants us to work together in pairs to practise some dialogues. If there is a new play, he asks us to decide on which part we would like to play. Otherwise he expects us to start rehearsing our current play. He always advises us to imagine the characters we represent. Last week he warned us not to speak too fast. After one hour he allows us to take a break. Afterwards he expects us to pay attention again. He is a great director! I hope to learn a lot from him.

**Exercise 3** (Seite 32)

1. Mrs Wilson has to go to the supermarket to buy some butter.
2. Why are you always the last one to come home?
3. Tell me when to be home.
4. Do you think it is very difficult to learn Chinese?
5. Thomas has told me how to get to the new library.
6. It was not easy for Peter to accept the part/role of the crazy postman.
7. Jenny is helping her parents (in order) to be allowed to go out in the evening.
8. What would be the best book (for me) to give (to) Anne?

**Exercise 4** (Seite 32)

1. Mr Wilson was angry to hear that the price of petrol had risen again.
2. Richard would be foolish not to invite Jenny to the party.
3. Jenny was happy to find/to have found these jeans in the sales.
4. Is it a problem for you to come earlier?
5. You will get a lot of exercises to do over the weekend.
6. Neil Armstrong was the first man to walk on the moon.

## 3.3 Infinitive or Gerund?

**Exercise 1** (Seite 34)

Peter: "Our teacher told us not to forget to read Shakespeare's Macbeth over the Easter holidays."
Jenny: "Now I regret missing the play on TV last week. I stopped reading after the scene in which the king is murdered, so I don't know the ending."
Peter: "So you must remember to take the book with you on our trip. I'll try to remind you."

Jenny: "But that means reading Shakespeare instead of having fun!"
Peter: "Well, then stop complaining and start reading/to read."
Jenny: "O.K. Although I prefer watching the play to reading it."

**Exercise 2** (Seite 34)

1 h) Sorry, I don't remember talking to you.
2 f) Don't forget to close the windows.
3 g) Thomas is really good at playing the guitar.
4 j) Jenny is interested in listening to Richard's story.
5 a) Would you mind helping your mother in the kitchen?
6 i) Jenny is looking forward to meeting Richard again.
7 c) Please remember to call me tomorrow.
8 e) Peter hadn't meant to make his father angry, so he apologised.
9 d) Jenny and Anne would like to go to the disco tonight.
10 b) Mr Wilson was tired, so he stopped to drink a cup of coffee.

**Exercise 3** (Seite 35)

1. Peter enjoys playing football, whereas he hates playing/to play basketball.
2. What kind of music do you like to listen/listening to? – I love listening/to listen to classical music, which sometimes means buying expensive CDs.
3. You must stop worrying about your problems and start to solve/solving them.
4. Do you know how to waltz? – Mum tried to teach me, but I am really bad at dancing. It's no use trying again.
5. If you cannot win the match, try developing a new strategy!
6. Don't forget to take this book back to the library. Do you remember paying the extra fee last month?
7. Thomas, are you interested in painting? – Sorry, but I prefer playing the guitar to painting.
8. Jenny and Peter are looking forward to performing a modern comedy next week.

## 3.4 The Participle

**Exercise 1** (Seite 37)

1. The people looking <u>for me</u> are my parents.
2. The person cutting <u>your hair</u> is doing a marvellous job!
3. The pizzas served <u>at the new restaurant</u> are great.
4. The woman living <u>next door</u> is my science teacher.
5. Science, the subject taught <u>by her</u>, includes chemistry, biology and physics.*
6. The example given <u>below the text</u> is difficult to understand.
7. The painter teaching <u>here last year</u> has gone to the south of France.
8. The man praising <u>Peter for his excellent performance</u> is his football coach.
9. The car damaged <u>by Peter's friend Tim</u> yesterday has a broken mirror now.*

* Da ein Partizip **nur** an die Stelle solcher Relativsätze treten kann, deren Subjekt das Relativpronomen bildet, müssen die Relativsätze in 5 und 9 vor dem Ersetzen ins Passiv umgeformt werden!

**Exercise 2** (Seite 38)

1. While translating the text, Thomas had to look up several words in the dictionary.
2. (Having been/Being) asked to bring his favourite book, Peter chose *Harry Potter*.
3. Having finished their homework, Jenny and Anne went swimming.
4. Mrs Wilson found Jenny's earring while cleaning the bathroom.
5. Arriving home, Jenny noticed that she had lost her key.
6. Being angry, Mr Wilson left his office.
7. Although expecting the test, Peter didn't do his homework properly.

## 3.5 Infinitive or Participle?

**Exercise** (Seite 39)

Mrs Wilson tells her husband what she saw, heard and smelt while she was walking their dog Rex: "When I closed the door, I heard our neighbour, Mr Patel, singing in the bathroom. At the same time, I saw his wife leave the house, get into her car and drive off in a hurry. Further down the street I heard Mrs Wright, the opera singer, practising, when I saw her son kissing his girlfriend behind a tree. Crossing the main street, I could hear several people arguing. Then I saw someone slam the front door and run away. Only a few minutes later I noticed a police car approaching. I felt my heart beating faster. I watched the policemen enter the house. But soon everything became quiet again. So I could continue my walk with Rex. Arriving at the park at last, Rex was happy smelling all the other dogs running around, and I enjoyed listening to the birds chirping in the trees."

## Test your Progress

**Exercise 1** (Seite 40)

1. Inviting Richard to the party means introducing him to all your friends.
2. It's no good staying up all night if you have to get up in the morning.
3. Anne was the only one to think the latest *James Bond* film was boring.
4. Did you enjoy spending the weekend in the mountains?
5. Thomas finally succeeded in being invited to perform at the Cavern Club.
6. His friend Daniel wants Peter to visit him in Munich next summer.
7. Do you find it difficult to learn German, Jenny?
8. Thank you for walking the dog!

**Exercise 2** (Seite 40)

1. Mrs Wilson likes reading/to read detective stories, so why not give her an Agatha Christie novel as a present?
2. Have you ever watched Dad trying to play ice hockey?
3. Jenny, you must remember to remind Anne that she will be responsible for feeding the cat next weekend.
4. Listen to Jenny singing! She hopes to win the song contest.
5. We can begin eating/to eat without waiting for Dad; he will be late today.
6. You must avoid getting into a traffic jam because we are invited to join the party at our neighbours'.

7. Richard, would you like to come to my birthday party? Don't worry about how to get home, my father will take you.
8. I could see you smoking. It's no use lying.
9. Playing football is great, especially after being at school till 3 pm.

**Exercise 3** (Seite 41)

1. Having closed/After closing the door behind them, the girls sat down to talk.
2. While listening to her favourite singer, Jenny tried to do her maths homework.
3. Thomas went to the travel agency, having been told to fetch some catalogues.
4. Although (being) treated fairly by his German teacher, Peter didn't like her.
5. Thomas happily accepted the holiday job offered to him.
6. Mr Wilson went to the delicatessen, wanting to prepare a special dinner.
7. Having spent all his pocket money, Peter asked Thomas to lend him £ 10.

**Exercise 4** (Seite 41)

Thomas is introducing his new girlfriend to his parents:
"This is Lisa from Cardiff. In her free time she likes playing/to play the drums in her band and sometimes enjoys reading historical novels. Lisa's sister teaches her how to take really beautiful photos with her digital camera. Lisa doesn't mind helping her little brother with his homework. She is keen on going to clubs, but rarely during the week because she can't stand being too tired to get up the next morning. She has decided to study medicine after her A-levels and wants to become a surgeon. She dreams of travelling to foreign countries and even considers working abroad for a couple of years as a doctor."

**Exercise 5** (Seite 42)

1. Our football coach has considered introducing new rules.
2. Jenny is used to singing at the youth club.
3. The doctor told you to stop smoking.
4. The new book written by John Grisham is a bestseller again.
5. I heard the door bell ring three times, so I knew it was Jenny.
6. Mrs Wilson wants Thomas to lay the table today.
7. Are you also looking forward to spending your holidays in New England in the USA?
8. Please remember to feed the dog tomorrow.
9. Peter was disappointed about not winning the match.

## 4.1 Singular and Plural

**Exercise 1** (Seite 45)

five apples
one kilo of flour
a packet of washing powder
one bar of chocolate
two bottles of milk
one chicken
half a pound of butter

**Exercise 2** (Seite 45)

1. Have you got any homework today?
2. The United States is bigger than Germany.
3. Our weekend trip was terrible because we had awful weather and the furniture in our hotel room was very old and run down.
4. Mum, can you help me? I need some advice.
5. Listen to the news. – What is it about?
6. Peter, your hair looks terrific!
7. Measles is quite a serious illness for old people.

**Exercise 3** (Seite 46)

3 T-shirts
3 pairs of shorts
2 pairs of jeans
2 sweaters
1 pair of pyjamas
4 pairs of socks
1 tracksuit

**Exercise 4** (Seite 48)

1. The Wilson family have been discussing their holiday plans for three hours now.
2. Dad is worried because his wages have decreased since last June.
3. The audience is/was (seltener: are/were) very interested in the journalists' presentation.
4. The management of my firm is going to announce the results of the tests tomorrow.
5. Jenny thinks the youth club is great fun.
6. Jenny's black leggings are too small.
7. Peter needs three new pairs of shorts.
8. This is the second pair of jeans you have bought this week.
9. Who knows where the scissors are? And where are my glasses?

## 4.2 Definite and Indefinite Article

**Exercise 1** (Seite 50)

| | |
|---|---|
| Jenny: | I'm so tired. I don't want to go to – school today. |
| Mrs Wilson: | Well, it's already – Friday! So take a shower and eat the breakfast I've prepared for you, and you will survive! |
| Jenny: | But I don't feel like – cereal and – milk today. |
| Mrs Wilson: | Take it or leave it, but hurry up! I don't want you to be late for – history again. |
| Jenny: | Oh, we will only talk about the society of the Middle Ages. |
| Mrs Wilson: | Isn't it interesting what – life was like then? |
| Jenny: | Well, I would prefer sleeping and dreaming of my own life. |

**Exercise 2** (Seite 52)

1. Staying at the Hilton costs £ 110 a night.
2. Anne always talks of becoming a teacher.
3. During her holidays, Jenny is going to work as a waitress.
4. Mr Wilson cannot go to work because he has a headache.
5. You've got an hour and a half/one and a half hours to write the essay.
6. Are you going to take a bath this evening?
7. It takes half an hour to get to the city centre.
8. You are not allowed to drive a car without a driving licence.

**Exercise 3** (Seite 52)

1. Could I have a glass of – water?
2. – Women do not always use – make-up.
3. Do you like the make-up I bought yesterday?
4. – Children love – Christmas.
5. What a good essay that is!
6. Are you going to – church – next Sunday?
7. I've never been to the British Museum.
8. Your collegue is a Hindu, isn't he? What does he eat for – lunch?
9. Have you ever visited the Millers on – Green Street?
10. Did you know the performance would be without a break?

## Test your Progress

**Exercise 1** (Seite 53)

1. Mrs Wilson: "Peter, are you going to wear these jeans today? They need washing soon."
2. We are going on a field trip today. Our class are meeting at the station.
3. Our teacher says physics is/will be easier to understand outdoors. But all the equipment has to be carried along.
4. Don't forget the scissors. We'll need them.
5. Is your team complete? The second group leaves/will leave in ten minutes.
6. People don't want to be disturbed!
7. Oh dear, I forgot my sunglasses! Now the sun is shining, so I need them.
8. If I had taken along my swimming trunks, I could have worn them for a swim in that nice lake.
9. When we got back to our school, the police were asking questions. They were looking for witnesses to an accident.
10. Our homework is to fill in this worksheet.

**Exercise 2** (Seite 53/54)

1. Are you feeling better? Can you go to – school tomorrow?
2. Have you tried the bread from the new bakery?
3. My favourite subject is – biology.
4. I have to go to the hospital to show Anne her homework.
5. We usually meet at – Piccadilly Circus before going to the cinema.
6. Did you know that Tim plays the trumpet?
7. Mary's father is a doctor.

8. I can't concentrate because I have a headache again.
9. Today we had to write an essay about – pollution.
10. Do you know anything about the history of the Middle Ages?

**Exercise 3** (Seite 54)

1. I was so tired yesterday. I only saw half the film.
2. You must not enter the room without the permission of the boss.
3. Have you seen my red leggings. I can't find them.
4. I need more information about holiday jobs.
5. When you come to London, you must visit – Buckingham Palace.
6. I have spent all my pocket money on two pairs of sunglasses.
7. Thomas, you must not be late three times a week.
8. Have you got – homework today?
9. The United States is very important for Germany's export industry.
10. Peter is a player in the local football team.

## 5.1 Kinds of Adverbs

**Exercise** (Seite 57)

After having landed at Rome International Airport**, the Wilsons are confidently looking for their transfer bus to the hotel. On their way through Rome* they are amazed about the unexpectedly bustling traffic. "Luckily, I do not have to drive here. I have never seen such traffic chaos! Rome is an extraordinarily lively city," Mr Wilson admits.

As the bus is pretty crowded, they are really glad to arrive at their hotel*. The entrance hall is elegant and brightly lit. A friendly young man receives them cordially at the reception desk* and congratulates Mrs Wilson with a bottle of champagne, then he hands the room keys over to her.

While they are waiting for the lift to the fifth floor*, Jenny is watching all the well-dressed people surrounding them. Peter isn't absolutely sure whether the man just entering the hall is the famous Italian football star Luca Toni. And Thomas is apparently attracted to the group of beautiful Italian girls standing over there and chatting cheerfully.

What a brilliant start into a promising Italian holiday!

| manner | place/direction | time/frequency | degree | comment |
|---|---|---|---|---|
| confidently<br>unexpectedly<br>brightly<br>cordially<br>well<br>cheerfully | here<br>over there<br>at Rome International Airport*<br>on their way through Rome*<br>at their hotel*<br>at the reception desk* | then<br>just<br>never<br>after having landed at Rome International Airport*<br>while they are waiting for the lift to the fifth floor* | extraordinarily<br>pretty<br>really<br>absolutely | luckily<br>apparently |

* Hierbei handelt es sich um adverbiale Bestimmungen *(adverbials)*, die nicht aus Adverbien, sondern aus Präpositionalgruppen bestehen.

** Hier verbergen sich gleich zwei adverbiale Bestimmungen: Der gesamte (!) Nebensatz fungiert als temporale Adverbiale, die Präpositionalgruppe at Rome International Airport außerdem als lokale.

## 5.2 Position of Adverbials

**Exercise 1** (Seite 59)

| Front-Position | Mid-Position | End-Position |
|---|---|---|
| adverbials of <u>comment</u><br>actually, apparently, fortunately, hopefully, obviously, of course, probably, unfortunately, in my opinion, … | adverbials of <u>indefinite time</u><br>soon, just, still, ever, already, later, once …<br><br>adverbials of <u>indefinite frequency</u><br>often, sometimes, always, never, usually, rarely, hardly, … | adverbials of <u>manner</u><br>beautifully, carefully, quickly, well, slowly, fantastically, …<br><br>adverbials of <u>place</u><br>here, there, upstairs, outside, everywhere, at the shop, in Rome, …<br><br>adverbials of <u>definite time</u><br>today, tomorrow, tonight, yesterday, in the year 2000, two years ago, next week, since/for …<br><br>adverbials of <u>definite frequency</u><br>daily, weekly, once, twice, every year, on Sundays, … |

**Exercise 2** (Seite 59)

1. I sometimes wear special clothes for my job.
2. I often work at weekends.
3. I usually work with my hands.
4. My job is really creative.
5. I often work outdoors.
6. I hardly work with animals.
7. In fact, you have to be strong. (oder: You have to be strong, in fact.)
8. You do not need a university degree at all.

Solution: The job described here is the job of a gardener.

**Exercise 3** (Seite 60)

*Lösungsvorschlag:*

1. Mr and Mrs Wilson sometimes go to a musical in London.
2. Jenny has never been in Italy before.
3. Thomas always liked pizza when he was child.
4. I often eat fish on Fridays.
5. You will soon see the Swiss Guard at the Vatican.
6. Mr Wilson rarely listened to classical music ten years ago.

**Exercise 4** (Seite 60)

1. Unfortunately, Mr Wilson does not speak Italian very well.
2. The Wilsons' guide Marco has lived happily in Rome for twenty years.
3. Jenny likes Italian ice-cream very much.
4. Mrs Wilson sometimes makes a delicious Italian cappuccino for herself.
5. Unfortunately, Thomas is late for the sightseeing tour.

6. Hopefully, you will enjoy/have enjoyed the meals at our restaurant.
7. Unfortunately, the Wilsons have (had) to walk upstairs in the evening because the lift does (did) not work properly.
8. Apparently Peter has eaten too much deliciously prepared pasta.

## Test your Progress

### Exercise 1 (Seite 61)

1. In fact, Jenny was allowed to go to the disco next to the hotel with Thomas yesterday.
2. Actually there were a lot of young Italian people there.
3. Fortunately, they met some nice people there, who could also speak English.
4. However, it was really funny when Thomas tried to talk to a (really) pretty girl in Italian.
5. Luckily, the music was not too loud, so they did not have to shout at all.
6. Of course, Jenny danced quite a lot.
7. Thomas especially liked the modern Italian music that was played before midnight.
8. Jenny and Thomas would really like to go there again on Saturday.

### Exercise 2 (Seite 62)

1. Mr Wilson locked their safe carefully and left the room.
2. The chambermaid always changes the bedclothes on Saturdays and Wednesdays.
3. Crossing the street in front of their hotel, Mrs Wilson almost had an accident.
4. "Dad, have you ever been to Rome?"
5. They have already decided to take the guided tour through the *Forum Romanum*.
6. "Mum and Dad, we'll see you at the restaurant at eight o'clock."
7. "We must really leave now!"
8. Obviously Peter is looking forward to visiting the Colosseum.

## 6.1 Phrasal Verbs

### Exercise 1 (Seite 64/65)

| Phrasal Verb | Bedeutung | Übersetzung |
|---|---|---|
| *break down* | when a car stops going | eine Panne haben |
| *break in* | 1. commit burglary<br>2. wear new shoes until they are comfortable | 1. einbrechen<br>2. *(neue Schuhe)* einlaufen |
| *break off* | discontinue | abbrechen |
| *bring up* | raise | *(Kinder)* aufziehen |
| *calm down* | become quiet | sich beruhigen |
| *carry on* | continue | weitermachen |
| *carry out* | perform | durch-/ausführen |
| *clear up* | tidy up: Please clear up this mess! | aufräumen |
| *drop off* | Could you drop me off at the hotel? | *(jmdn. mit dem Auto)* absetzen |
| *fill in* | complete | *(Formular)* ausfüllen |
| *find out* | discover | herausfinden |
| *get away* | escape | entkommen |
| *get back* | return | zurückkehren |
| *get off* | leave (a vehicle) | (aus einem Fahrzeug) aussteigen |
| *get on* | 1. enter (a vehicle)<br>2. continue | 1. (in ein Fahrzeug) einsteigen<br>2. weitermachen |
| *get up* | rise: I got up at 9 am today. | aufstehen |

| Phrasal Verb | Bedeutung | Übersetzung |
|---|---|---|
| *give away* | 1. give as a present<br>2. reveal *(a secret)* | 1. ver-/herschenken<br>2. preisgeben, verraten |
| *give in* | surrender: Do not give in to him! | nachgeben |
| *give up* | 1. surrender: Are you giving up?<br>2. stop *(doing sth.)* | aufgeben, kapitulieren<br>aufgeben, aufhören mit |
| *go ahead* | continue | weitermachen |
| *go on* | 1. continue: Go on with it!<br>2. happen: What's going on here? | 1. weitermachen<br>2. geschehen |
| *grow up* | become an adult | aufwachsen |
| *hang on* | wait | warten |
| *leave out* | omit | aus-/weglassen |
| *look after* | Kate is looking after little Jim tonight. | *(z. B. auf Kinder)* aufpassen |
| *look for* | search (for) | suchen |
| *look out* | watch out, pay attention | aufpassen |
| *look up* | check in a book | nachschlagen |
| *make up* | invent | erfinden |
| *put off* | delay, postpone | (auf später) verschieben |
| *put on* | What dress should I put on tonight? | anziehen |
| *put up* | put up a cupboard/a building | aufstellen, errichten |
| *ring off* | hang up | (Hörer) auflegen |
| *run away* | leave suddenly | weglaufen |
| *run down* | get empty | leer werden |
| *run out (of)* | run out of peas/peas have run out | fast keine mehr haben/ausgehen |
| *set off* | leave, get on one's way | aufbrechen |
| *speak up* | speak louder | lauter sprechen |
| *take off* | 1. remove *(clothes)*<br>2. leave the ground | 1. ausziehen<br>2. abheben *(Flugzeug)* |
| *throw away* | get rid of | wegwerfen |
| *try on* | put on to see if it fits | anprobieren |
| *turn down* | 1. lower the volume<br>2. reject: Why did he turn down this offer? | 1. leiser stellen<br>2. ablehnen |
| *turn off* | 1. change direction<br>2. press a button to stop sth. | 1. abbiegen<br>2. ausschalten |
| *turn up* | 1. appear: He turned up late last night.<br>2. increase the volume | 1. auftauchen<br>2. lauter stellen |
| *wake up* | 1. arouse so. from sleeping<br>2. stop sleeping | 1. aufwecken<br>2. aufwachen |
| *work out* | calculate | herausfinden, errechnen |
| *write down* | make a note | aufschreiben, notieren |

**Exercise 2** (Seite 66)

1. Mr Wilson will be late for dinner because his car has broken down.
2. Everything is very dusty in the attic. Don't forget to put on old clothes.
3. Peter must work out the costs for his new furniture.
4. The drilling machine is too loud, I can't hear you. Speak up!
5. The electric screwdriver doesn't work. The batteries have run down.
6. Jenny, you've been talking on the phone for half an hour. Ring off now and start helping us!
7. If the paint doesn't dry till tomorrow, we must put off our further plans.
8. I'm not ready yet. Hang on a minute.
9. What's that noise? What is going on in the living room?
10. After getting the missing tools from the hardware store, Thomas can drop you off at the youth club.

**Exercise 3** (Seite 67)

1. I have to go and get some more wooden boards; get on/go on/carry on with your work while I am away.
2. Peter and Thomas are arguing and neither of them wants to give in.
3. Have you seen Rex? I have (already) looked for him everywhere.
4. Read the instructions properly and then carry them out.
5. When Jenny was late for work yesterday, she tried to make up an excuse.
6. Can you please help me to put up this cupboard?

## 6.2 Collocations

**Exercise 1** (Seite 68/69)

**make**

- ... a coffee – Kaffee machen
- ... friends – Freundschaft(en) schließen
- ... a mess – Unordnung machen
- ... a cake – eine Kuchen machen/backen
- ... a phone call – ein Telefongespräch führen
- ... an appointment – einen Termin vereinbaren/sich verabreden
- ... a decision – eine Entscheidung treffen
- ... money – Geld verdienen
- ... a mistake – einen Fehler machen
- ... a good impression – einen guten Eindruck machen
- ... the bed – das Bett machen
- ... up your mind – sich entscheiden

**do**

- ... your homework – die Hausaufgaben machen
- ... the washing-up – das Geschirr spülen/den Abwasch erledigen
- ... damage – Schaden anrichten
- the shopping – Einkäufe machen/die Einkäufe erledigen
- ... the cooking – kochen
- ... your best – dein Bestes tun/geben
- ... nothing – nichts tun
- ... the cleaning – putzen
- ... (something) for a living – (mit etwas) den Lebensunterhalt verdienen
- ... the ironing – bügeln/die Bügelwäsche erledigen
- ... someone a favour – jemandem einen Gefallen tun
- ... well – gut abschneiden

**Exercise 2** (Seite 69)

1. The Wilsons have made the decision that Peter may move into the attic room.
2. Peter has to look for a holiday job to make some money for his new furniture.
3. Can you do me a favour and prepare some sandwiches, Jenny?
4. I'm going to clean the windows after doing my homework.
5. Thomas, can you do the shopping today?
6. I have made an appointment with an architect for tomorrow to ask him if we can tear down this wall.
7. Peter, if you do well in your next maths test, we will pay for you new furniture.
8. Thomas has already made friends with the owner of the do-it-yourself store.

**Exercise 3** (Seite 70)

| | | |
|---|---|---|
| tap | potatoes | mashed potatoes |
| scrambled | water | tap water |
| roast | salad | fruit salad |
| sparkling | beef | roast beef |
| fruit | coffee | white coffee |
| herbal | beans | baked beans |
| mashed | eggs | scrambled eggs |
| baked | water | sparkling water |
| white | tea | herbal tea |

**Exercise 4** (Seite 70)

1. blow the whistle (= pfeifen)
2. qualify for the championship (= sich für die Meisterschaft qualifizieren)
3. deflect a shot (= einen Schuss abfälschen)
4. fail to score (= nicht treffen)
5. score a goal (= ein Tor schießen)
6. take the lead (= in Führung gehen)
7. commit a foul (= foulen)
8. make a substitution (= einen Spieler auswechseln)
9. hit the post (= den Pfosten treffen)
10. take a free kick (= einen Freistoß ausführen)

**Exercise 5** (Seite 71)

Last weekend Peter's favourite football team, Chelsea, had an important match to qualify for the next championship. Only four minutes after the referee had blown the whistle, the new striker scored a goal and his team took the lead. But then one of the defenders committed a foul outside the penalty area, so the other team took a free kick. Luckily, the ball hit the post! Although their coach made two substitutions, they didn't score a goal. And when the referee blew the final whistle, Peter was happy with his team winning!

**Exercise 6** (Seite 71)

| **... the computer** | **... a (computer) file** | **... an e-mail** |
|---|---|---|
| crash ... | open ... | get ... |
| shut down ... | delete ... | open ... |
| play on ... | create ... | reply to ... |
| reboot ... | back up ... | check ... |
| | | delete ... |
| | | send ... |
| | | receive ... |

## 6.3 Idioms

### Exercise 1 (Seite 72)

| | |
|---|---|
| to be like chalk and cheese | to be completely different |
| something makes your mouth water | something makes you want to eat it |
| not for all the tea in China | not even for a great reward |
| to have a sweet tooth | to love eating sweet things |
| to bear fruit | to have good results |
| a big cheese | an important and powerful person |
| to be the best/greatest thing since sliced bread | to be fantastic |

### Exercise 2 (Seite 72)

1. Mr Lang, our neighbour, never goes out to meet people; he is **a lone wolf**.
2. Anne's cousin Jill is **as busy as a bee** and **as sly as a fox**.
3. Having done most of the work by himself, Peter is **as proud as a peacock**.
4. You don't have to be afraid of Mr Lang. He **wouldn't hurt a fly**.
5. The new owner isn't able to run that business. I'm afraid it will **go to the dogs**.
6. After the alarm they were all in a panic and **running round like headless chickens**.
7. The workers didn't get much of the profit because the management took **the lion's share**.
8. Jenny was so nervous, she **had butterflies in her stomach** when she met Richard.

### Exercise 3 (Seite 73)

1. Jenny and Anne are very good friends. They **get on like a ...**.
   a) **house on fire** b) burning house c) fire in the house
2. Thomas **hit the ...** when Peter told him that he had broken his bike.
   a) wall b) **roof** c) floor
3. Jenny, why don't you listen to me. It's like **talking to a ...**.
   a) wooden door b) metal fence c) **brick wall**
4. Peter wanted to build a balcony, but without enough money, his plan **went out of the ...**
   a) chimney b) **window** c) door
5. This terrible noise of the drilling machine **is driving me ...**.
   a) up the stairs b) out of the house c) **up the wall**
6. Mr Wilson **smokes like a ...**. He must give up smoking.
   a) fireplace b) cooker c) **chimney**

### Exercise 4 (Seite 73)

1. This wall painting will be **the icing on the cake** in your new room, Peter!
   das Tüpfelchen auf dem i
2. If you buy the wooden boards on your way home, you can **kill two birds with one stone**.
   zwei Fliegen mit einer Klappe schlagen
3. Cleaning the windows is **not** really **my cup of tea**.
   nicht mein Fall
4. It was just a minor mistake, so don't **make a mountain out of a molehill**!
   aus einer Mücke einen Elefanten machen

5. When Mrs Wilson is talking to his teachers, Peter would like to **be a fly on the wall**.
   Mäuschen spielen
6. Anne's new hockey coach is even worse than the one before. The team got **out of the frying pan into the fire**.
   vom Regen in die Traufe
7. Jenny **acts as a guinea pig** in an experiment for a school project.
   spielt Versuchskaninchen

## 6.4 False Friends

**Exercise** (Seite 75)

1. Don't be afraid. Our dog Rex won't hurt you. He is always good (= brav).
2. I can't find (= finden) Thomas! – How do you like (= findest) him? – I think (= ich finde) he has become a decent (= anständiger) young man.
3. Have you heard the current (= aktuellen) weather forecast?
4. He doesn't get enough pension (= Rente) to pay his rent (= Miete).
5. Old people can be very sensitive (= sensibel).
6. Could I have (= bekommen) a glass of white wine, please?
7. Let's have a look at the map (= Landkarte) before we get lost.
8. Have you always been such a committed (= engagierter) football player?
9. Our grammar school (= Gymnasium) has a big new gymnasium (= Turnhalle).
10. I'll give you my mobile phone (= Handy) if you want to call him.

## Test your Progress

**Exercise 1** (Seite 76)

1. I can't hear anything. Can you turn the music up a bit?
2. Unfortunately Richard had to put off his party until next month.
3. My grandpa is almost deaf, so you really have to speak up!
4. Finally, Mr Wilson will give up smoking.
5. I can't believe her. I think she has made the whole thing up.
6. Hiking in these new shoes wasn't a good idea. I should have broken them in.
7. Babysitting isn't an easy job if you have to look after three little children.
8. Can you drop me off at the library on your way to the office?
9. Don't tell your little brother, or he'll give away our secret again.
10. He got a great offer, so why did he turn it down?

**Exercise 2** (Seite 76)

1. Have you made a decision?
2. My computer doesn't work properly. I have to reboot it.
3. Peter's team took the lead.
4. The coach had to make two substitutions.
5. You got all the points in your test. Well done!
6. I'd like a cup of white coffee.
7. Unfortunately, the ball has hit the post.
8. This e-mail might contain a virus, so you had better delete it.
9. Have you done all your homework?
10. They made friends 30 years ago.

**Exercise 3** (Seite 77)

1. On my birthday I am having a pool party with cocktails, and these artificial palm trees will be the icing on the cake!
2. When Jenny told her mother that she had taken her new necklace, Mrs Wilson almost hit the roof.
3. I would never do a bungee-jump, not for all the tea in China.
4. I have underestimated Mr Miller. He is as sly as a fox.
5. Our old English teacher, Mrs Peters, was very strict, but with Mr Black we got out of the frying pan into the fire.
6. If you are talking about your problem all the time, you are making a mountain out of a molehill.
7. For Thomas a car of his own would be the best/greatest thing since sliced bread.
8. With the new chef you can hardly eat at that restaurant any more. I'm sure it will go to the dogs.
9. This kind of modern art isn't really my cup of tea.
10. You have worked hard, and eventually your efforts will bear fruit.

**Exercise 4** (Seite 78)

1. This is a current report dealing with the financial crisis.
2. Yesterday he gave me that lovely ring. Now we are engaged.
3. If you want to keep on living here, you have to pay your rent on time.
4. Anne's mum is pregnant. She is going to have a baby.
5. What do you think is the right decision?
6. My skin is very sensitive. I have to be careful.
7. Possibly I'll come for a short visit, but I'm not sure yet.
8. Listen, if you are good and tidy up your room, you will get some ice-cream afterwards.

## 7.1 American Indians

**Exercise 1** (Seite 80)

**Wounded Knee**

| | true | false | not in text |
|---|---|---|---|
| 1. The Indian Removal Act said that the American Indians had to sell their land. | | ✔ | |
| 2. In 1876, all Native Americans were sent to reservations. | ✔ | | |
| 3. The Native Americans didn't want European food because they hadn't known it before. | | | ✔ |
| 4. In their reservations the Native Americans couldn't find enough animals for hunting. | | | ✔ |
| 5. The "Ghost Dance" was a war dance. | | ✔ | |
| 6. The US government sent soldiers because they were afraid of an attack by the Native Americans. | ✔ | | |
| 7. Wounded Knee was an Indian leader in South Dakota. | | ✔ | |

| | true | false | not in text |
|---|---|---|---|
| 8. Within five minutes, about three hundred American Indians were killed by soldiers. | ✔ | | |
| 9. The Native Americans stopped their protest after the massacre. | ✔ | | |

**Exercise 2** (Seite 81)

*Lösungsvorschlag:*

1. What happened in 1830?
   In 1830 President Andrew Jackson passed the *Indian Removal Act*, a law that made it possible for the government to buy land from the Native Americans.
2. What happened to many of the 100,000 Native Americans on their way to Oklahoma?
   Many of them became sick or died.
3. In what respect were the Native Americans' children separated from their traditional life?
   They were sent to boarding schools, where they were not allowed to learn about their own culture or speak their own languages.
4. What was the big problem in the year 1890?
   The Native Americans couldn't grow food because the weather was too hot and there wasn't enough rain.
5. What did the soldiers originally want to do in South Dakota in 1890?
   They wanted to stop the dancing and move the Indians further south to Nebraska.
6. How many people lost their lives in the Wounded Knee Massacre?
   About 300 Sioux Indians and 25 US soldiers lost their lives.
7. Why can the Wounded Knee Massacre be seen as a turning point in the history of intercultural relations in North America?
   It can be seen as a turning point because it was the last armed conflict between Native Americans and US soldiers.

**Exercise 3** (Seite 81)

*Lösungsvorschlag:*

1. American Indians had lived in North America long before the first European settlers/the first Europeans/the first people from Europe arrived.
2. In 1876 the rest of the American Indians had to move to reservations because the US still needed more land.
3. The Native Americans began to protest because they didn't have enough food and life was impossibly hard. (auch: ... (because) they had to send their children away to boarding schools and were not allowed to live according to their own traditions.)
4. The peaceful "Ghost Dance" sometimes lasted for three or four days.
5. The American people were shocked when they heard the news about the Wounded Knee Massacre/ ... the news that the soldiers had killed/massacred 300 Native Americans within five minutes.
6. After the massacre the American Indians gave their guns/weapons to the soldiers.

**Exercise 4** (Seite 82/83)

*Lösungsvorschlag:*

1. What rights were written down in the Indian Removal Act?
   - the government's right to buy land from the American Indians
   - the American Indians' right not to sell/to refuse to sell their land
2. Why did the Indians take part in the "Ghostdance"?
   - because the living conditions were unbearably hard
   - they used the "Ghostdance" as part of a peaceful protest
   - they hoped they could live in peace with the settlers from Europe
3. How did the Wounded Knee Massacre come about?
   - There were rising conflicts when soldiers wanted the Indians to hand over their guns.
   - It was a difficult situation, and people on both sides were getting nervous.
   - Suddenly, the shooting started, with a disastrous result.
4. In what respect have the Native Americans left their mark on the map of the USA?
   - Many state names are derived from Indian words, for example Oklahoma, Kentucky or Michigan.

**Exercise 5** (Seite 83)

| | |
|---|---|
| give someone the right to do something | – allow someone (to do) something |
| take/send someone away from a place | – remove someone from somewhere |
| make someone do something | – force someone to do something |
| without war and fighting | – in peace, peaceful |
| conflicts/fights with words | – arguments |
| killing in which many people die on one side | – massacre |
| the people of a country | – nation |
| using weapons | – armed |

## 7.2 National Parks

**Exercise 1** (Seite 84)

*Lösungsvorschlag:*

The text is about the creation of the first national park, the initial problems, the park rangers and the further development of national parks.

**Exercise 2** (Seite 84/85)

**National Parks**

In the 19th century, industry was expanding in the US. America wanted to protect its beautiful countryside, and in 1864, it became the first country in the world to officially do this. President Abraham Lincoln signed an important law that said nature areas should only be used for recreation and that they should be open for everyone to use. This law created something the world had never seen before – national parks.

The very first one was Yellowstone National Park. It was created on March 1st, 1872, and is located in the western states of Wyoming, Montana and Idaho. The park is home to wildlife like grizzly bears, wolves and bison. And there are about 600 species of trees and plants there! Around 2.8 million visitors come to Yellowstone every year to see the world's most famous geyser, 'Old Faithful'. Every 90 minutes, the geyser shoots up to 32,000 liters of hot water into the air.

Yellowstone is big – it has an area of 8,983 $km^2$. Back in 1872, there were no formal park regulations for visitors. Also, there weren't enough park helpers, and the first park manager worked for five years for free because there wasn't enough money to pay him. The lack of money made it very difficult to protect the park, and very often people stole natural resources and hunted animals illegally. Soon the US government realized that it had to do something. It provided money for the world's first park ranger, Harry Yount. But Harry left a year later – he said the job was too difficult for one man. Almost ten years later, in 1886, they called in the army to help look after the park.

The army managed the park for an amazing thirty-two years! It developed regulations for the protection of the park. And thanks to the army, many species of wildlife were saved from dying out. In 1916, the army's job was finished, and they gave control of the park to a new organization – the National Park Service (NPS). Today park rangers are an important part of the NPS: they report forest fires and stop people from damaging the park. They can also carry guns, like the police. Park rangers have their own uniforms and they wear hats called 'Ranger Stetsons', which are much like the old army hats.

Including Yellowstone, there are 58 national parks in the US today. Famous national parks include Badlands National Park in South Dakota, Yosemite National Park in California, Grand Canyon National Park in Arizona, and Rocky Mountain National Park in Colorado. And far-away states like Alaska and Hawaii also have their own national parks. Some people say that national parks were the best idea America ever had. And other countries thought so too, so today there are national parks all over the world.

**Exercise 3** (Seite 86)

*Lösungsvorschläge (natürlich können andere Formulierungen auch richtig sein):*

1. Why had it become necessary in the $19^{th}$ century to protect nature?
   - Industry was growing, factories were spreading/built all over the landscape/throughout the country.
2. What was the law Abraham Lincoln signed in 1864 about?
   - the creation of national parks
   - special natural areas for recreation
   - these areas should be open for all people
3. What is Yellowstone National Park famous for?
   - It was the very first national park.
   - It is famous for the geyser 'Old Faithful'.
   - amazing flora and fauna/many different (kinds of) animals and plants
4. What problems had to be solved during the first years of Yellowstone's existence?
   - lack of official regulations for visitors
   - lack of money
   - lack of park helpers to protect the park
   - therefore illegal hunting and theft of natural resources
5. What was the army needed for, and what did they achieve by 1916?
   - When the first park ranger had left after only one year, the army was called to take care of the park.
   - The army introduced regulations to protect the park.
   - The army helped to save many species from extinction.
6. Why are park rangers, according to the text, so important for the national parks?
   - They inform people about forest fires.
   - They stop people from violating regulations.
7. In what respect was the idea of national parks not only a national achievement?
   - The idea spread from the US to foreign countries.
   - Today national parks exist all over the world.

## 7.3 American English versus British English

### Exercise 1 (Seite 89)

American English word for BE *rubbish bin*: trash can

| | | | | | | | | | |
|---|---|---|---|---|---|---|---|---|---|
| flat | A | P | A | R | T | M | E | N | T |
| lorry | | | | T | R | U | C | K | |
| rubber | | | E | R | A | S | E | R | |
| petrol | | | G | A | S | | | | |
| crisps | | | | C | H | I | P | S | |
| sweets | | | | | C | A | N | D | Y |
| autumn | | | | F | A | L | L | | |
| queue | | | L | I | N | E | | | |

### Exercise 2 (Seite 89)

1. San Francisco is my favorite city in the States. I would like to have an apartment there.
   San Francisco is my favourite city in the States. I would like to have a flat there.
2. Yesterday I went to the movie theater instead of watching a soccer game on TV.
   Yesterday I went to the cinema instead of watching a football match on TV.
3. We are planning a barbecue in our back yard for next week. Would you like fries with your steak?
   We are planning a barbecue in our back garden for next week. Would you like chips with your steak?
4. Have you seen the new candy store? They have lots of different cookies.
   Have you seen the new sweetshop/sweet shop? They have lots of different biscuits.
5. When I was in 7th grade, I always had good grades.
   When I was in year 7, I always had good marks.

### Exercise 3 (Seite 90)

| | BE | AE |
|---|---|---|
| That street was really dirty, with garbage everywhere. | | ✔ |
| Tom was standing in a queue waiting to get into the lift. | ✔ | |
| What is your favourite song? | ✔ | |
| I couldn't go to the theatre yesterday. | ✔ | |
| They know all about it because I already spoke to them. | | ✔ |
| You must not park on the pavement. | ✔ | |
| Last night I dreamed of a new car. | | ✔ |
| The mailbox is over there on the right, in front of the drugstore. | | ✔ |
| Mr Black lives on the first floor, so he needn't climb up any stairs. | | ✔ |
| Did you see the new catalog yet? | | ✔ |

## Test your Progress

**Exercise 1** (Seite 91)

British English word for AE *downtown*: city centre

| | | | | | | | | | | | |
|---|---|---|---|---|---|---|---|---|---|---|---|
| movie theater | | | | | | C | I | N | E | M | A |
| railroad | | | | R | A | I | L | W | A | Y | |
| mail | | | P | O | S | T | | | | | |
| mean | | N | A | S | T | Y | | | | | |
| backpack | | | | R | U | C | K | S | A | C | K |
| pants | T | R | O | U | S | E | R | S | | | |
| yard | G | A | R | D | E | N | | | | | |
| schedule | | T | I | M | E | T | A | B | L | E | |
| freeway | | M | O | T | O | R | W | A | Y | | |
| sidewalk | | | P | A | V | E | M | E | N | T | |

**Exercise 2** (Seite 91)

1. You can take the underground [to the] city centre*.
   You can take the subway downtown*.
2. I have already spelt my name twice.
   I already spelled** my name twice.
3. Do you like the new flavour?
   Do you like the new flavor?
4. When I was young, his flat was above the shop.
   When I was young, his apartment was above the store.
5. Our new car needs less petrol.
   Our new car needs less gas.
6. In the 21st century you cannot stop globalisation any more.
   In the 21st century you cannot stop globalization any more.

* downtown = (to the/in the/at the) city centre
** je 1 Punkt für spelling und tense (American English: already + simple past)

**Exercise 3** (Seite 92)

Dear Jenny,
Up to now our holiday here in California has been fantastic. Yesterday we visited Yosemite National Park. It is open all year round, but in autumn, when the colours of the leaves are incredibly impressive, most of the visitors come here for hiking. The most spectacular rock here is called 'Half Dome' and it is more than 2,500 metres high. Perhaps you have already seen it in a film?
In the park you have to be very careful about black bears. You must not throw away any rubbish because they smell and look for everything from leftover biscuits to empty beer tins. But with the right behaviour you can enjoy the beauty of nature in Yosemite Park.
You must come here and see it all by yourself!
Yours, Linda

## 8.2 Crossword Puzzle
(Seite 96)

phrasal verb for *to chase (so.)*: come after (so.)

| | | | | | | | | | | | | |
|---|---|---|---|---|---|---|---|---|---|---|---|---|
| to be as proud as a ... | | | P | E | A | C | O | C | K | | | |
| phrasal verb for *to reject* | T | U | R | N | D | O | W | N | | | | |
| English word for *engagiert* | | | C | O | M | M | I | T | T | E | D | |
| synonym for *to give in* | | S | U | R | R | E | N | D | E | R | | |
| ... wine (with bubbles of gas) | | | | S | P | A | R | K | L | I | N | G |
| "... your shoes before you come in!" | T | A | K | E | O | F | F | | | | | |
| AE word for *toilet* | | | R | E | S | T | R | O | O | M | | |
| famous national park in the USA | | | Y | O | S | E | M | I | T | E | | |
| phrasal verb for *to tidy* | | C | L | E | A | R | U | P | | | | |

## 8.4 The Wilson Family's Board Game
(Seite 98)

1. I am going to do my homework tomorrow.
2. I didn't know that Tim was such a fool.
4. Mr Wilson enjoys telling jokes.
5. She loves cookies.
6. Richard hasn't been at the youth club since last weekend.
7. I'm afraid the batteries are running down.
9. Thomas has never been to the USA.
10. We won't go on holiday if you are ill.
11. Who wants to do the shopping today?
13. We met at the club at 8 o'clock.
14. Listen! The police are coming.
15. This trip has been the best thing since sliced bread.
16. Jenny has not called Anne yet.
17. Today children learn to respect – nature.
18. The man standing there is my uncle.
21. The USA is really great!
22. I think I'll get/receive/be given a bike for my birthday.
23. If you worked hard, you would pass the test.

## Bild- und Textnachweis

**PantherMedia:** S. 15 © Petra Wenzel
**Photocase:** S. 35 © Yvonnes_photos; S. 46 © suze; S. 63 © mathias the dread
**Shutterstock:** S. 5 © Vinicius Tupinamba; S. 11 © Jeff Dalton; S. 13 © kristian sekulic; S. 34 © Feverpitch; S. 43 © Wheeler Images; S. 47 © Monkey Business Images; S. 66 © ZanyZeus; S. 77 © Jan Schuler; S. 89 © Norebbo; S. 106 © Sam Chadwick; S. 107 © photosani
**www.fotolia.de:** S. 21 © patrick roth; S. 22 © Jean-Paul Demolin, S. 25 © gajatz; S. 28 © Stefan Körber; S. 40 © HelleM, S. 41 © iofoto; S. 44 © william CASEY; S. 48 © jaeggimedia; S. 50 © Torsten Schon; S. 52 Mitte © Christos Kyratsous; S. 52 unten © fazon; S. 55 © Mirec; S. 57 © claire cordier; S. 59 © Sternstunden; S. 61 © DWP; S. 79 © Sharon Day; S. 83 © Ralf Müller; S. 84 © Nate; S. 86 © michael langley; S. 87 links © pics on stock; S. 87 rechts © kerstinR; S. 90 © Marcin Wasilewski; S. 92 © Jose Gil; S. 93 © Carmen Steiner; S. 94 © Katarzyna Cielecka; S. 102 © starekase; S. 109 © Beth Van Trees; S. 110 © Danny Hooks; S. 117 © Ben Smawfield
**Texte** S. 82 und 84 f./122 f.: Simon Tribe, Stralsund, aus: *English Network: Pocket America.*

# Index

Zusätzliche Übungen mit Lösungen zu jedem Kapitel findest du auf unserer online-Lern-Plattform www.gute-noten-in.de

Mit deinem Passwort für Englisch, Klasse 8, kannst du dich ganz einfach kostenfrei einloggen und üben:

**dKh63V**